Praise for *Zen for Christians*

"Kim Boykin writes in the skilled language of simplicity. While addressing those new to Zen, she offers practical wisdom, challenge, and encouragement to all practitioners."

—Rose Mary Dougherty, Shalem Institute for Spiritual
Formation, Bethesda, Maryland

"The great religions of the world have much to learn from each other. Kim Boykin's book is a skillful step in that direction. The heart of the matter of Zen is presented in a direct and informative way that is based on her firsthand experience of Zen training. This should prove to be a helpful guidebook for any Christian who wishes to explore Zen practice."

—John Daido Loori, Roshi, Abbot, Zen Mountain Monastery

"This lovely, wise, and practical introduction to Zen keeps its promise of companionship as the kind of spiritual cookbook you can bring right into the kitchen. Recipe-reading like this, in fact, inspires you to get into the kitchen, encourages you to keep at it, and invites you to share your efforts in communion with others."

—Steven Tipton, coauthor, *Habits of the Heart*

Zen for Christians

a

beginner's

guide

Kim Boykin

Foreword by Gerald G. May

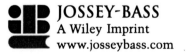

JOSSEY-BASS
A Wiley Imprint
www.josseybass.com

Published by Jossey-Bass
A Wiley Imprint
989 Market Street, San Francisco, CA 94103   www.josseybass.com

Jossey-Bass books and products are available through most bookstores. To contact
Jossey-Bass directly, call our Customer Care Department within the United States
at (800) 956-7739, outside the United States at (317) 572-3986, or fax (317) 572-4002.

Jossey-Bass also publishes its books in a variety of electronic formats. Some content that appears in print may not be available in electronic books.

Meditation postures photos: Copyright 1998 Skip Nall; courtesy of MKZC
Publications, *Beginning Zen (A Sourcebook for the Spiritual Path)*
Buddha photo courtesy www.siamese-dream.com
Hotei photo courtesy Joanne Clapp Fullagar

Library of Congress Cataloging-in-Publication Data
Boykin, Kim
  Zen for Christians : a beginner's guide / Kim Boykin ; foreword by
Gerald G. May.
      p. cm.
Includes bibliographical references and index.
      ISBN: 978-0-470-90751-1
  1. Spiritual life—Zen Buddhism. 2. Christianity and other
religions—Relations—Zen Buddhism.
  3. Zen Buddhism—Relations—Christianity.
  4. Boykin, Kim 5. Spiritual biography. I. Title.
  BQ9288.B69 2003
  261.2'43927—dc21   2002154862

FIRST EDITION
HB Printing   10 9 8 7 6 5 4 3 2 1

Contents

To Brian

Foreword

I wish I'd had this book when I began to explore Buddhism. It would have made things much easier. My first experience with Zen was like a spiritual boot camp—entirely unpleasant. The teacher barked orders, and his students tried desperately to get everything exactly right. There was never any relief from the intensity, no breath of humor. It's true that sitting Zen can have its unpleasant times no matter how it's presented. As a popular American Buddhist saying goes, "A mind is a terrible thing to watch." But the mind can also be hilarious, and Zen should have its lighter side as well. Nowadays I am suspicious of any spiritual teaching that lacks humor, but then I was just beginning. Like the other students in that first class, I believed that something good would happen only if I could get everything perfectly right. But all I felt was pain and frustration, so I assumed I was doing something wrong. I was a failure.

It would have been so nice to have this book then, to touch into Kim Boykin's gentle encouragement and good humor and to hear her assurance that getting things right is not the point at all. But I would have to wait; it was 1972, and Kim Boykin was far from her own first Zen sitting.

Like many Americans who explore Buddhism, I had a fairly solid background in traditional Western religion. My Methodist parents made sure I said my prayers and went to Sunday school. I knew the stories of Jesus and even felt I had a close personal relationship with him. As I got older though, I grew first frustrated and then angry about what I saw as hypocrisy in the people of my church. Not only did they often use their religion as an excuse for moral arrogance, but they also resisted any questioning of beliefs. They didn't seem to want any part of going deeper in the spiritual life.

I did not understand why, but I definitely wanted to go deeper. As an adult, I searched for a local church that would welcome my wonderings, and found none. I looked for a religious community that would teach me about the inner spiritual life, about prayer and meditation, and found none. So when I began to explore Eastern religions, I carried some baggage with me. Church, as I knew it, had failed to meet my needs, and I was taking my spiritual business elsewhere. Or so I thought.

What surprised me, eventually, was that my foray into Buddhism led me in a kind of circle, back to my Christian roots. Over time, Buddhist practices somehow revealed to me the rich resources of Christian contemplative tradition that had been there all along, hidden beneath the busyness of popular religion.

I was not alone in that experience. Over my thirty years of working with the Shalem Institute, I met many people who felt that their churches and synagogues were lacking in spirituality.

Most nurtured a simple, wistful longing for "something else."
They were not clear about exactly what they wanted, but they
knew they were hungry. In their searching, many turned
toward the East and experienced exactly what I had—an even-
tual discovery of deep nourishment within their own original
tradition. The phenomenon happened so frequently that we
gave it a name: "pilgrimage home."

It is here in this pilgrimage home that resources such as
this book become crucially important; they provide guidance
and nourishment that are not easily found elsewhere. For a person beginning a conscious interior spiritual journey, it may not
be easy to tell where the true nourishment can be found. As a
society, we have been inundated with quick-and-easy recipes
for spiritual and psychological self-help. Although many of
these are well intentioned, they often fail to provide the real satisfaction people are seeking. A quick drive-through at a fast-
food restaurant may ease one's hunger for a while, but it takes
a carefully, lovingly cooked meal to nourish the deeper places in
a lasting way.

In this regard, Kim Boykin is a good cook. In this book
(which she herself likens to a cookbook), she serves up nutri-
tious recipes that will stick to your ribs. In the text of the book,
Kim shares the story of her own pilgrimage. It is perhaps
because of her unusual religious background that she is able
to remain free of the negative "baggage" that so often creeps
into religious discussions. She has no particular ax to grind with
any religion, no psychological agenda to impose on the reader.

She is able to present her material simply, clearly, and directly, with a lightness and humor that immediately put one at ease.

At the same time, she is not afraid to tackle the thorny questions that inevitably arise when Christians look at Zen. What are the similarities between Zen and Christianity, and what are the differences? What does it really mean for a Christian to practice Zen Buddhism? Does it amount to a denial of one's Christian faith, or can it lead to a deepening of it?

Kim addresses such questions more coherently and revealingly than any other writer I know, and she teaches Zen practice with the greatest clarity and lightness I have seen anywhere. This is truly good nourishment. I only wish I'd had it when I began.

Bethesda, Maryland   Gerald G. May
February 2003   Senior Fellow, Shalem Institute
          www.shalem.org

Zen for Christians

An Invitation to Zen Practice

Zen for Christians is a beginner's guide to Zen, written especially for Christians. It weaves together detailed instructions in Zen meditation, an introduction to the teachings of Zen, and reflections on Zen in relation to Christianity. It is based on the introductory classes on Zen that I've been teaching for the past five years at churches and in evening adult education programs.

"Zen for Christians" does not mean Zen *adapted* for Christians in the way that "yoga for pregnancy" means yoga adapted for pregnant women. The Zen in this book is just plain Zen, but the presentation of Zen in this book is especially for Christians. I tell the story of my own experience with Zen and Christianity. I address issues of particular interest and concern to Christians. And I explore some of the similar observations that Zen and Christianity make about the experience of being human.

Zen is a way of liberation from suffering—both the suffering we experience ourselves and the suffering we cause others. It is a practical and experiential tradition, centered in a form of meditation that can be practiced by people of any or no religion. Zen practice is about opening compassionate aware-ness to all of reality and realizing that the joy and freedom we long for are available right here and now, in the midst of the messiness and pain and confusion of our lives.

Zen is a way of selflessness, in two senses of the word. First, Zen is a way of directly experiencing what Buddhism calls "no-self"—realizing that the distinction between "me" and "not me" isn't so clear and definite as we usually assume it is and experiencing the interconnection and interdependence of all things. Second, Zen is a way of selflessness as opposed to self-ishness—a way of being helpful instead of harmful, a way of compassion for everything and everyone, including ourselves. These two forms of selflessness are connected. As we more fully experience reality from the perspective of no-self, we are freed from the tyranny of an illusory "self" and freed for a life of self-less joy and compassion.

Zen is a peculiar religious tradition. Many people wouldn't call it "religious" at all. Zen is not about doctrines or beliefs. It's not about worship or devotion. Zen is not theistic, but it isn't athe-istic either, or even agnostic. Zen simply doesn't address the subject of God. In Zen, the Buddha is not understood to be a god or messiah or superhuman but an ordinary human being who discovered a way of liberation from suffering and taught this way to others.

Trappist monk Thomas Merton says that comparing Zen and Christianity is like comparing tennis and mathematics. I think Zen and Christianity are more comparable than that (and Merton probably does too, since he says this in *Zen and the Birds of Appetite,* which is full of comparisons of the two traditions), but I *would* say that practicing Zen as a Christian is like playing tennis as a mathematician. If you're a mathematician and you want to play tennis, you just keep on being a mathematician and you also play tennis. There's no special trick to it. You don't need to wear shorts and tennis shoes to do your mathematics, and you don't need to ponder differential equations while playing tennis. If you're a Christian and you want to practice Zen, you just keep on being a Christian and you also practice Zen.

Christians have found that Zen practice can be a powerful way to nurture our capacity to love God, our neighbors, and ourselves, and our capacity to say to God from the heart and in all circumstances, "Thy will be done"—not my will, but thine. In particular, Zen practice can be a powerful way to help us see and let go of what gets in the way of loving God and all of God's creation and what gets in the way of opening to God's will.

Of course, the Christian tradition offers us its own spiritual practices to nurture our capacity to love God and creation and to open to God's will. In this book, I simply offer Zen as another spiritual practice that you might wish to try. I invite you to incorporate Zen practice into your life as a Christian, as many Christians, both lay and ordained, Protestant and Catholic, have already done.

Since Zen is fundamentally a practice—something you do, something you experience—the essentials of Zen cannot be grasped by reading about it. In this way, Zen is like any activity that you learn through practice and experience, like playing tennis or driving a car or baking bread. You can get some useful and interesting information by reading about it, but it is by getting out on the court and hitting some tennis balls, by getting in the car and driving, by kneading the dough and letting it rise, that you learn how to do it and what it's really all about.

Reading this book, then, is like reading a cookbook. The recipes in a cookbook are there not just to read but to guide you in preparing something to eat. In this book, the practice sections are the recipes, and the chapters help you better understand the recipes and more fully appreciate the cuisine. The list of recommended resources at the end of the book tells you where to learn more about this cuisine and where to get ingredients that you won't find at your local supermarket. I invite you to try some of the recipes—not just to read about the tastes and textures and aromas of Zen but to experience them for yourself.

Practice

Zazen: Counting the Breath

The Japanese word *zen* means meditation, and the central practice of Zen is *zazen,* or sitting meditation, also simply called "sitting." This book includes instructions in three slightly different forms of zazen, as well as several other forms of meditation. We will begin with a basic Zen meditation practice called counting the breath.

Getting Ready

Find a relatively quiet place, where you can sit undisturbed. Eventually, you will be able to do zazen in almost any environment, but especially in the beginning, a quiet space is helpful. If possible, the lighting should be dim, like twilight.

Wear comfortable, loose-fitting clothes. You don't want to be wearing anything that constricts your breathing, so if you are wearing pants that are snug at the waist, you might want to undo the top button and loosen your belt. Remove your shoes. Either socks or bare feet are fine.

You will need a cushion that is several inches thick when compressed. Try a bed pillow folded in half or a rolled-up blanket, or try putting a sofa cushion on the floor and sitting on the edge of it.

If you want to make zazen a regular practice, I would recommend getting a *zafu* or a *seiza* bench to sit on. A zafu is a round meditation cushion, about a foot in diameter and about six inches thick, traditionally black or brown, stuffed with a plant fiber called kapok. A recent variation is a zafu stuffed with buckwheat hulls. A seiza bench is a small wooden bench, about six to eight inches high, used to support a kneeling position. (Benches of the same sort can be found at Christian retreat centers, where they're called prayer benches or kneeling benches.)

The zafu or seiza bench is traditionally placed on top of a *zabuton,* a thick, squarish mat that cushions the knees and legs. For cross-legged positions a carpeted floor is usually sufficient cushioning, but for kneeling positions it's helpful to have extra cushioning. A blanket or two folded in half several times can function as a zabuton.

The only equipment you need for Zen practice is something good to sit on, though catalogues of Buddhist supplies and ads in Buddhist magazines will try to sell you all sorts of other stuff. The list of recommended resources at the back of the book includes sources of zafus, zabutons, seiza benches, and other supplies.

Finding a Sitting Position

You need to find a sitting position that allows you to have an upright spine and to be stable, still, and relatively comfortable. Zen meditation is not a matter of the mind only but of the whole person, the whole body-mind. An alert posture supports an alert mind, and an alert mind supports an alert posture.

The cross-legged positions have been time-tested for millennia as excellent positions for meditation—*if* you can get into one of them with some degree of comfort. One position that works well for many people is the so-called Burmese position, in which both calves rest on the floor in front of you, parallel to one another and not actually crossed (see Figure 1). If you're fairly limber, you might try the half-lotus position, in which one calf is on the floor and the other calf is pulled up so that the foot rests on the opposite thigh (see Figure 2). This position torques the spine just a bit to one side, so if you mainly sit in the half-lotus position, it's a good idea to switch which calf is on top occasionally so that the spine gets torqued to the other side sometimes. For those who are exceptionally limber, the classic meditation posture is the full-lotus position, in which each foot rests on the opposite thigh (see Figure 3). This is the most balanced and stable position, but I know very few Zen practitioners who regularly sit in a full lotus, which most people find impossible or painful, even with practice.

In any of the cross-legged positions, sit on the front half of the zafu so that it acts as a sort of wedge under you, raising your buttocks off the floor while allowing both knees to touch the floor. If one or both of your knees don't reach the floor at first, that's fine. If you regularly sit in a cross-legged position, you'll loosen up over time.

A cross-legged position that you should *not* use is an ordinary "Indian-style" or "tailor" position, in which the calves are crossed, with both feet on the floor and both knees in the air. This position is not conducive to sitting up straight, and the circulation in the legs is cut off too easily.

You can also use a kneeling position, which many people find more comfortable than a cross-legged position. Kneel with your knees apart and your feet on either side of the zafu, and sit down on the front half of the zafu. If you want more height, turn the zafu on end. This way, your knees will not be bent at such a sharp angle, but you may feel a little more precariously balanced. Or you can use a seiza bench. Kneel; put the seiza bench so that its legs are on either side of your calves and the seat slants down toward the front; and sit on the bench (see Figure 4).

You can also sit in a chair. Sit with your back upright and your feet firmly planted on the floor, about shoulder-width apart. Do not lean against the back of the chair (see Figure 5). It will be easier to maintain your posture if you put a zafu (or your makeshift zafu) on the seat of the chair to act as a wedge so that your thighs slant down from hip to knee instead of being parallel to the floor. If you don't have a cushion that will create this slant of the thighs, I would recommend putting a small cushion between the chair back and your lower back to lean against and help keep your back upright.

Figure 1. Burmese Position.

I encourage you to experiment with various sitting positions to see what works best for your body. But please do not try to force your body into positions that will put stress on weak or injured hips, legs, or knees!

In all of the sitting positions—cross-legged, kneeling, or sitting in a chair—tilt the top of your pelvis forward so that there is a curve in your lower back, with your abdomen protruding in front and your buttocks protruding in back. (Notice that this is exactly the opposite of a slouch, in which the top of the pelvis is tilted back.) The forward tilt of the pelvis and the curve of the lower back help keep the back upright with minimal effort from your muscles. And the downward slant of the thighs from hip to knee helps keep the pelvis tilted forward.

Sit with your spine long and tall, upright but not stiff. Imagine that you're pushing up the sky with the crown of your head or that you're a marionette on a string that pulls straight up from the top of your head. The energy that goes into sitting upright is all in the spine. Let everything else be loose and relaxed. The abdomen is relaxed. The shoulders are relaxed down and back. I sometimes feel like I'm a big laundry bag, with everything hanging in a loose, heavy lump from the drawstring pulling up at the top.

Figure 2. Half Lotus.

Figure 3. Full Lotus.

The head is upright, with the chin tucked slightly in and down, not jutting forward or lifted up. Viewed from the side, the ears are in a vertical line with the shoulders.

The mouth is closed (unless you're congested and are having trouble breathing through your nose), with the tongue pressing lightly against the roof of your mouth to inhibit salivation.

There is a special hand position, or *mudra,* used in zazen. Take your dominant hand—your left hand if you're left-handed or your right hand if you're right-handed—and place it in your lap, palm up. Place the other hand on top of it, palm up, with the middle knuckles approximately overlapping, and touch your thumbs lightly together so that your hands form an oval.

Let your hands rest in your lap, up against your abdomen, and let your arms hang loosely, with no tension in your arms or shoulders.

The eyes are kept open in zazen. This helps prevent drowsiness and supports awareness of the here and now. Let your gaze fall at about a 45-degree angle, resting on the floor three to four feet in front of you. Let your eyelids be relaxed and droopy, and let your gaze be relaxed and somewhat unfocused. At some Zen centers and monasteries, you sit facing a wall, in which case you look "through" the wall to rest your gaze at an imaginary point three to four feet in front of you.

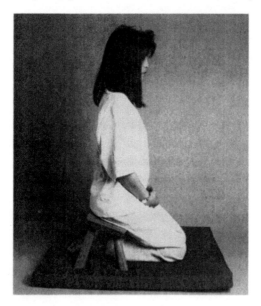

Figure 4. Kneeling.

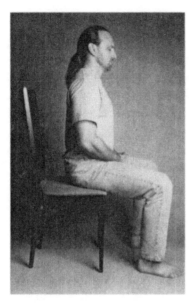

Figure 5. Sitting in a Chair.

You maintain this posture in complete stillness for the entire meditation period—no rearranging your legs, no fidgeting, no scratching your nose, no cracking your back—no moving at all. Let the body be still and quiet. Zen teacher Charlotte Joko Beck says that zazen is basically "a simplified space." We sit completely still in a quiet and dimly lit place to simplify our space—to minimize stimuli—and give ourselves an opportunity to see what's happening in the present moment and what our minds get involved with instead of the present moment.

You may feel some discomfort sitting in a zazen posture for more than a few minutes. Be assured that it becomes easier over time, as the muscles get used to sitting up straight and, if you're sitting cross-legged, as the muscles and joints loosen up. As unlikely as this may sound at first, these postures really are, in the long run, the most comfortable way to sit upright and still for an extended period. If you sit several periods in a row, as is done at Zen centers, you may want to change your position from one period to the next, to shift the stress on your body—perhaps simply shifting which leg is in front in the Burmese position or which leg is on top in the half-lotus position.

You may find that one or both of your legs fall asleep when you sit cross-legged. Sitting a bit further forward or back on the cushion may prevent this. If you're sitting in a half lotus, adjust the foot that's underneath so that it presses into the opposite thigh and calf as little as possible. If your legs do fall asleep, just let them be asleep. Unless you already have some trouble with your legs or hips, no harm will come from having your legs asleep for a five-minute or thirty-five-minute sitting period. At the end of the sitting period, be sure that some feeling has returned to your legs before you try to stand up, or you might collapse right back down to the floor.

Awareness of Breathing and Thoughts

Once in a sitting position, you may find it helpful to take one or two slow, deep breaths to settle in. Then let your breathing be however it is—fast or slow, deep or shallow, regular or irregular—not manipulating it in any way.

Become aware of your breathing—the physical sensations of your breathing. Let your attention settle in your *hara,* a point about two inches below the navel, understood in Zen to be the physical and spiritual center of the body. Feel your breathing from the hara. Feel the expansion of the abdomen as you inhale and the contraction of the abdomen as you exhale.

Starting with the inhalation, begin silently counting your inhalations and exhalations. Count the inhalation "one," exhalation "two," inhalation "three," and so on. If you get to ten, start again at one. When you realize that your attention has wandered away and you've lost track of the counting, notice the thought you were involved with—or the most recent thought in a long series of thoughts—and gently return your attention to the breathing, starting the count again at one. The word *thought* here is meant broadly to include any mental activity: ideas, emotions, images, plans, memories, fantasies, judgments, whatever. If thoughts arise and then vanish without carrying your attention away from the counting, you don't need to start again at one; just continue counting. If you realize that you've counted past ten, start again at one.

That's all there is to it. Notice the thought that captured your attention, and gently return your attention to the breathing, starting the count again at one. Notice the thought, return to the breathing, notice the thought, return to the breathing— over and over and over.

The point of this practice isn't to count to ten without a thought. If you repeatedly notice your wandering thoughts and return your attention to the breathing after counting just one breath, that's great. If there can be said to be a point to counting the breath, it is to practice returning to the present moment. You repeatedly notice the thoughts that carry your attention away and return your attention to the physical sensations of the breathing, which is always happening right here and now. Thoughts are fine. They are an intrinsic part of Zen practice. They are what you return *from*.

Zazen does not require exertion. You don't need to tense your muscles or grit your teeth or cling onto your breath for dear life and try to keep thoughts from arising. As you can discover for yourself, that's futile anyway. Zazen simply requires persistence—a commitment to noticing thoughts and gently returning your attention to the breathing, again and again and again.

How Long and When to Sit

When you're beginning, I'd suggest sitting for five to ten minutes, once or twice a day. If, after a few weeks or a few months, you find that you'd like to sit longer, then increase your sitting a little bit at a time—say, doing one more sitting period a day or adding five minutes to your sitting periods. It is not advisable to sit for more than about forty minutes at a time. If you want to sit longer than that, you can alternate periods of sitting meditation with brief periods of walking meditation, as described in the next practice section.

To time my sitting periods, I place a clock just at the edge of my field of vision and check it now and then. I would not recommend using an alarm clock or a kitchen timer because the noise is indeed an alarming way to end a sitting period. You can buy a tape or CD on which a bell rings to start the period, then there's a certain length of silence, and then another bell rings to end the period; or you can make a tape or CD like this yourself. Or you can use incense made to burn for certain lengths of time, so that your sitting period is over when the incense has burned out.

It is better to sit regularly for a short time than every once in a while for a long time, and it is good to sit every day or nearly every day. It is helpful to sit at about the same time each day so that zazen becomes a habit, a part of your daily routine. The only time that isn't very good for zazen is right after a meal, when you're likely to be drowsy and dull. First thing in the morning and last thing at night are times that work well for many people, but you'll need to find what works with your own rhythms and the rhythms of your household.

The Essentials of Counting the Breath

- Find a sitting posture that allows you to have an upright spine and to be stable and completely still.
- Keep your eyes open, with your gaze lowered at about a 45-degree angle, soft-focused, eyelids droopy.

- Take one or two slow, deep breaths. Then let your breath be however it is.

- Let your attention settle in your *hara* (about two inches below the navel).

- Starting with the inhalation, begin counting your inhalations and exhalations silently to yourself: one, two, three, . . . If you get to ten, start again at one.

- When you realize that your attention has wandered away and you've lost track of the counting, notice the thought and gently return your attention to the breathing, starting the count again at one. (If thoughts arise but don't carry your attention away from the counting, just continue counting.)

Notice the thought,
   return to the breathing,
      notice the thought,
         return to the breathing,
            notice the thought,
               return to the breathing, . . .

Disengaging the Clutch

Here is an image of what happens in zazen.

The engine of the mind is constantly spinning, and off our attention goes, all over town, all over the country, even crossing borders into other countries. In zazen, we practice isengaging the clutch. We practice shifting into neutral, letting our attention coast to a stop, and letting the mind idle.

Our usual way of dealing with life is to drive all over, hoping to find a place where everything suits us, where there is no pain, where we can be completely happy, or at least happier than we are now. Although we can indeed solve some of our problems by driving someplace else, or by taking a new route or stepping on the gas or slowing to a crawl, these strategies won't solve the fundamental problems of pain and death. No matter where we go or what route we take, no matter how fast we go or how slowly, we won't escape pain and death.

You probably already know, or at least suspect, that there's no escape, or you wouldn't be reading a book like this. You've tried to escape. You've tried the interstates. You've tried the back roads. You've tried going off-road in your SUV. You've tried higher-octane gas and new tires. You've tried riding a bicycle instead. But none of it worked. Pain and death kept on chasing you.

Oddly enough, the freedom we're looking for is found not in trying to flee this big mess we're in but in stopping right here in the middle of it.

In a Bible study group several years ago, I was struck by a passage from Isaiah that seems to express a similar insight:

In returning and rest you shall be saved;
*   in quietness and in trust shall be your strength.*
But you refused and said,

"No! We will flee upon horses"—
     therefore you shall flee!
and, "We will ride upon swift steeds"—
     therefore your pursuers shall be swift!

If we insist on fleeing, we will be pursued. If we flee swiftly, we will be pursued swiftly. Our salvation is found in returning and rest.

To rest from our fleeing, we don't need to shut off the car engine. We only need to disengage the clutch. When we disconnect the wheels from the engine, the car can stay right here, no matter how fast the engine spins. We don't need to quit having thoughts. We only need to notice the thoughts and let them go. Then our attention can stay right here, no matter how fast the mind spins. Of course, there's little reason to step on the accelerator while we're in neutral, so the engine does tend to slow down when we disengage the clutch.

So this is the practice: when we realize that we're driving away, we notice where we are and disengage the clutch. We notice the thought that captured our attention and gently return our attention to the breathing. Then, inevitably, without even noticing it, we engage the clutch and step on the gas and off we go. That's fine. That's exactly what human minds are prone to do. When we realize that we're racing off at seventy-five miles an hour, we notice where we are and disengage the clutch. We do this over and over and over: notice where we've driven and disengage the clutch.

With practice, we tend to get quicker, on average, at noticing where we've driven and disengaging the clutch. Instead of noticing, when we get to Nova Scotia, that we're not in Los Angeles anymore, we start to notice in New York. Then we start to notice in Chicago, in Denver, in Grand Junction, in Las Vegas. Now and then we notice as soon as we get on the highway or as we're pulling out of our own driveway.

But it doesn't matter when we notice where we've driven. It's the noticing and disengaging the clutch that's the key. Road trips are fine. Zen practice is about noticing when we're taking one and disengaging the clutch:

> *Notice where you've driven,*
>   *disengage the clutch,*
>   *notice where you've driven,*
>   *disengage the clutch,*
>   *notice where you've driven,*
>   *disengage the clutch, . . .*

1

How I Became a Christian Zen Practitioner

I grew up in Los Angeles, in no religious tradition. During my childhood, my mom was involved in the Unitarian Church on and off, and my dad was a Mormon for several years—this was after they'd divorced. I occasionally went to church with them. I liked the Unitarian church better because I could wear jeans and we did arts and crafts. For five summers, I went to a Unitarian summer camp where we tie-dyed T-shirts, sang folk songs, and played noncompetitive games, and the only rules were "Don't do anything that will hurt anyone else" and "Don't throw rocks." My grandmother, who became a born-again Christian late in life, taught me a few bedtime prayers and gave me a children's Bible that I never read. And at my private elementary school, we sang a little prayer before lunch, and we recited Luke's narrative of the birth of Jesus at the Christmas pageant. That about sums up my childhood religious training.

At Vassar College, in upstate New York, I majored in cognitive science, which included classes in psychology, computer science, philosophy, and linguistics. Initially, I focused on computer science, but midway through college, I began to lean toward the philosophical side of my major, and I also started taking religion classes.

When I read Freud, Marx, and Nietzsche, I thought they had religion pretty well figured out. Religion was a neurosis or the opiate of the people or the rationalization of weakness or something along those lines. That is, religion was something I didn't need to bother with personally, though I figured I should learn a bit about it as part of a well-rounded liberal arts education.

But then I started reading about the mystical and monastic traditions of Buddhism and Christianity, and I read William James's classic on the psychology of religion, *The Varieties of Religious Experience,* and I started to think that religion might have something to say to me after all. Both of my grandmothers had died during my sophomore year in college, which almost certainly contributed to my newfound interest in the deep issues of human life, though I made that connection only in hindsight.

In the fall of my senior year, my Buddhism class took a field trip one Saturday to Zen Mountain Monastery, in the nearby Catskill Mountains. I was intrigued by the monastery and felt a certain attraction to Zen, though I remember chatting with one of the monks and wondering how such a normal-seeming guy had ended up shaving his head and devoting his whole life to Zen. In the spring, the Zen teacher from the monastery came to Vassar to give a talk, and afterward I inquired about the possibility of doing a retreat at the monastery. My friend Anne and I spent our spring break that year at the monastery, following the rigorous monastic schedule of work and meditation.

Monastic life turned out to be different in many ways from my image of bald men in medieval robes, in complete silence, copying manuscripts by hand. For one thing, there are both women and men in residence at Zen Mountain Monastery. The monastery usually has twenty to forty full-time residents, which at the time included about five "monastics"—their gender-inclusive term for monks and nuns—and now includes about twice that number. The rest of the residents are there for a limited period of time agreed on in advance, anywhere up to a year, without making or necessarily intending to make any longer commitment. And there are usually some twenty to forty guests each weekend for retreats.

The abbot and senior teacher of the monastery, John Daido Loori, Roshi, is from New Jersey and was raised Catholic. (The title *Roshi,* which literally means "old master," is used for a Zen teacher whose awakening has been certified by his or her own Zen teacher.) He counts Saint Teresa of Avila and Saint John of the Cross among his spiritual teachers. His Zen teacher, Taizan Maezumi, Roshi, was from Japan and founded the Zen Center of Los Angeles.

When I made my first visit to the monastery, only two residents had shaved heads: the abbot and the head monastic. In the meditation hall, residents wear Japanese-style robes—gray for students, black for monastics, white for senior lay students. The rest of the time, they wear ordinary clothes in black or other dark or neutral colors so as to blend in with the rest of the *sangha,* or community.

A day at the monastery is spent mostly in work and meditation. The daily schedule varies slightly, depending on the season, but a typical day begins with wake-up at 4:30 A.M. and zazen at 5:00—two thirty-five-minute sitting periods separated by five minutes of walking meditation—and a twenty-minute service mainly involving a lot of chanting and bowing. The day includes seven and a half hours of work, three good vegetarian meals, and some time for rest and relaxation. And the day ends with another block of two sitting periods at 7:30 P.M. and lights-out at 9:30. Silence is generally kept from evening zazen through about 10:00 A.M. the next day. My favorite exception to this rule is that on Wednesday nights, cookies are served in the dining hall after evening zazen, and you can chat on "cookie night."

Like all newcomers to the monastery, Anne and I were taught the practice of counting the breath. I spent a lot of time noticing the noisiness of my brain and the complaints of my body about sitting completely still with a straight back, and I discovered the simple wonder of paying attention to what's actually happening. Immediately after doing zazen, I usually felt peaceful and relaxed, and I didn't feel much like talking or performing any unnecessary actions. But this was not a feeling of drowsiness or lethargy: I felt focused and alert and very aware of everything around me. During my whole stay at the monastery, but especially after zazen, I really enjoyed eating. Maybe this was simply because the food at the monastery was so much better than the food at school, but I think it was also because I was attending more than usual to the actions and sensations of eating.

The monastery supports itself by offering weekend and weeklong retreats, so a lot of the work of the monastery is that of running a retreat center. Guests are assigned a job each day, depending on what is needed—helping in the kitchen, housekeeping, gardening, lawn mowing, office work. Monastics and other long-term residents have an ongoing job. There's a head cook, an accountant, a work supervisor, a registrar, and so forth. The monastery residents don't make hand-illuminated copies of sacred texts, but they do make audiotapes and videotapes of Zen teaching and publish a quarterly journal, and one of the first things you notice in the office is all the computer equipment.

The monastery has the equivalent of a weekend, called *hosan,* from Sunday afternoon, after the weekend guests leave, through Tuesday afternoon. During hosan there is no schedule to follow and no rule of silence. Residents are on their own for meals, and you can leave the monastery grounds to go for a hike in the mountains or spend some time in New York City or just go to nearby Woodstock for ice cream. The television in the library is off-limits during the week but can be used during hosan. While Anne and I were visiting, a bunch of us watched a videotape of *Return of the Jedi.*

One week of each month is a *sesshin,* or intensive meditation retreat. During sesshin (pronounced "seh-*sheen*" or "seh-*shin*"), silence is kept at all times, and most of each day is spent in zazen.

Everything done at the monastery all day, all year, is part of the practice—not just zazen, but working, eating, even resting. And everyone there—monastics and laypeople, residents and guests—follows the same monastic schedule and discipline. The whole environment is designed to encourage and facilitate practicing at all times the awareness that is practiced in zazen: repeatedly noticing wandering thoughts and returning to full engagement with the present moment.

Several years after this visit to the monastery, I heard someone say, after some intensive Zen practice, that it felt like she'd had all the plaque scraped off her brain. That's how I felt at the end of my week's stay: like I had a fresh, clean, shiny brain. Especially for the first few days after leaving the monastery, I was more aware of all the meaningless and unnecessary chatter going on all the time—my own chattering, other people's chattering, and the incessant chattering in my brain. And I kept feeling like I was getting too much stimulation or doing too many things at the same time. As we drove away from the monastery at the end of the week, we were talking, listening to the radio, and watching the snow hit the windshield, and this seemed like two too many things to be doing at once, like this was more than one could fully attend to. Back at school, I found that I had an easier time taking care of tasks that I ordinarily would have put off or grumbled about.

Shortly after my college graduation in 1987, during a cross-country drive from New York to Los Angeles with my aunt and my college possessions, I became suddenly and painfully aware of my own mortality and finitude, my smallness and powerlessness in the universe. I recognized for the first time, in a gut way, that I would eventually die and that I wouldn't be consulted about whether that was OK with me. Like it or not, sooner or later, I *would* die. I felt terrified and confused, like my world had turned inside out. I wondered how people could so blithely go about their daily lives knowing that they were going to die. I felt as though now I really understood the existentialist philosophers I'd read in college, the "sick soul" of William James, and the story of the Buddha, a pampered, sheltered prince who was in his twenties before he discovered some of the fundamental realities of human existence: aging, illness, and death.

I suppose you might call this crisis a conversion experience, in that it decisively and permanently reoriented my life, propelling me on my religious search. But we usually imagine conversion experiences as joyful, and this experience was horrifying. I was glad, some years later, to read what Susan Howatch, author of a series of novels about the Anglican Church, says about her own conversion: "I felt as if God had seized me by the scruff of the neck, slammed me against the nearest wall, and was now shaking me until my teeth rattled." She adds, "Why people think a religious conversion is all sweetness and light I have no idea. It must be one of the big spiritual misconceptions of our time."

I spent that summer in Hawaii with my mom and stepdad, who were living there at the time, but I didn't much enjoy my exotic locale. I slept as much as possible—my preferred method of escaping myself and the world—and read anything that I thought might help me understand what was going on with me and what to do about it, mainly books on religious experience and meditation.

That fall, I moved to Boulder, Colorado, to start a Ph.D. program in philosophy at the University of Colorado. Boulder is a center for Tibetan Buddhism in the United States, and I began a regular meditation practice there, with the support of classes and weekend meditation retreats at the Naropa Institute (now Naropa University), a small college in Boulder founded by Tibetan Buddhist teacher Chögyam Trungpa. I also read some of the classics of the Christian contemplative tradition: *The Cloud of Unknowing,* Saint John of the Cross's *Dark Night of the Soul,* and Thomas Merton's *New Seeds of Contemplation.* I quickly discovered that philosophy wasn't going to address the Big Questions in a way that would satisfy me, and I sat in my philosophy classes wondering if the other students actually cared about the issues we were discussing and, if so, why. My undergraduate adviser had warned me that I wouldn't like graduate study in philosophy, and he was right. I dropped out of the Ph.D. program shortly after the start of my second semester.

By that point, my religious search was by far the most important thing in my life. The questions of life and death were urgent and painful and unrelenting, and I wanted to devote some time to single-minded, wholehearted spiritual practice. So I spent three months of the fall of 1988 at Zen Mountain Monastery, the monastery I had visited in college.

After that, I returned to Boulder and transferred into the graduate program in religious studies at the University of

Colorado, but I quickly became frustrated that no one seemed to want to talk about religion in relation to their own lives. They were observing religion from the outside, as anthropologists and sociologists, and I realized that I was primarily interested in exploring religion from the inside. At that point I didn't want to be reading and writing and talking about religion; I wanted to be practicing it. So I quit the religious studies program and went back to the Zen monastery, this time for a year's residency, beginning in the summer of 1989.

When I tell people that I lived at a monastery, they often say something like, "That must have been so peaceful." But *peaceful* is not one of the adjectives that comes to mind. I remember thinking that the schedule felt *relentless*. The experience was intense, challenging, difficult. I almost always felt sleep-deprived. I was only twenty-three at the time and was dealing with basic issues of growing up—work, relationships, and so forth—at the same time as questions about life and death. I once asked one of the monastics, "Don't you sometimes wish you believed in Someone you could pray to for help?" but he looked at me uncomprehendingly and said no. I learned a lot about myself during my time at the monastery but felt afterward that it might have been too much all at once.

My future husband Brian and I dated during my year's residency at the monastery. We had met two years earlier through the Buddhist community in Boulder, but we got together long-distance, writing letters while I was in New York and he was in Colorado, and he came out to the monastery three times to visit. Brian was teaching at the University of Colorado while finishing his dissertation in theology for the

University of Chicago. After my year at the monastery, I returned to Boulder to be with Brian—who had just finished a thirty-day silent retreat at a Jesuit retreat center. We got married two years later.

Although Brian is Boston Irish-Catholic and my background was Southern California agnostic, we somehow ended up with strikingly similar worldviews. When we moved in together, between the two of us we had no car, no couch, and no television, but we had two computers, three zafus, and five copies of *The Cloud of Unknowing* (in three different translations).

Toward the end of my time at the monastery and especially after I moved back to Boulder, I was really struggling with my Zen practice and my Zen teacher. On Thursday nights, Brian and I sat with a small Zen group that met in the basement of the Tibetan Buddhist center downtown, but that was all the Zen practice I was doing, and even that felt like a chore. At the monastery, I had realized that I had never had to work for much of anything in my life and had never done much of anything requiring discipline. School work had come easily; I was never involved in sports; I had quit piano lessons after a year and a half. And I was discovering that some of the most important things in life—spiritual practice and committed relationships—take work and discipline. I tended to give myself guilt trips about not sitting much, thinking things like, "What will help me be at peace is to sit, but I really don't feel like sitting, but by not sitting I'm contributing to my own unhappiness, and isn't that stupid." Naturally, this line of thinking didn't exactly inspire me to spiritual discipline. It just made me feel guilty on top of not being at peace.

I finally figured out that at least part of what I had been thinking of as existential angst or a "dark night of the soul" was garden-variety depression, so I started to see a therapist. But I didn't trust an exclusively therapeutic worldview, and I felt like I needed some sort of spiritual guidance also. Brian knew a Catholic nun who worked at the Jesuit retreat center where he'd done his thirty-day retreat, and he thought I'd hit it off with her. I did. I went to the retreat center every few months for a two- or three-day silent retreat and met with Sister Eleanor for spiritual direction. This didn't seem like a radical shift to me—talking about my spiritual life with a Catholic nun instead of a Zen teacher. I had been getting inspiration for my Buddhist practice from the Christian mystics all along, and Eleanor was happy to work with me even though I wasn't Christian. One welcome difference from the Zen monastery was that Eleanor encouraged me to relax and get lots of rest while I was on retreat.

A big part of my struggle with my spiritual practice was that I had smashed up against the limits of my own willpower. The style of practice at the Zen monastery at that time felt willful, effortful, goal-oriented, and that was my own approach to Zen practice. I thought it was all about pushing for *kensho*—an enlightenment experience, or "breakthrough"—but I hadn't had any breakthroughs. Buddhism is supposed to be about liberation from suffering, but I was still miserable.

Both Zen and Christianity teach that our liberation is not something we can earn or create or achieve, but it was in the Christian tradition, through my retreats with Eleanor, that I finally started to understand what this means. I had begun to recognize the vital importance of grace. I had begun to recognize that if my liberation depended on me or anything I did, it was hopeless.

Gerald May's *Will and Spirit,* a book on the psychology of contemplative spirituality, helped clarify my struggles and gave me some vocabulary for the "willingness" of true contemplative practice as opposed to the "willfulness" with which I had been practicing Zen. I had been trying to use my spiritual practice to get what I wanted, when spiritual practice is actually about being with reality as it is. I had been trying to satisfy my own will instead of opening to God's will. No wonder my practice had been such a struggle!

With this new insight into spiritual practice, I thought that now I could get back into Zen and practice willingness instead of willfulness. But whenever I started to think about it, I would immediately get caught up in thoughts about how it would be *good for me.* That is, I would immediately fall back into making my Zen practice an instrument of my will. So I decided I'd better give my Zen practice a rest for a while longer, since it seemed only to exacerbate my willfulness.

An insight I was missing at the time was that *of course* I would practice willingness willfully—that's natural and inevitable—and my willfulness could be treated like any other wandering thought that arises during meditation: notice the willful thought, and return my attention to the present moment. Notice, return, notice, return, notice, return—that's what Zen practice is. It was fine if I kept noticing myself thinking, "I *will* be willing!" But I didn't get that then.

I had told Eleanor, when I started doing retreats with her, that I could talk God language but had no idea what to do with Jesus. Tentatively, after many meetings, she suggested that I might want to try a little visualization: Imagine that Jesus is walking toward you. What do you do? She had intended for me to go off to the chapel or someplace later in the day and try this, but I did it right when she said it. I was in a high meadow in the Sierras, and a stereotypical Jesus, with beard and flowing robe and sandals, was walking toward me on a little path. As he got closer, I ran up to him, fell down at his feet with my arms wrapped around his ankles, and, crying, said, "I'm so glad you're here!" He would know exactly what I needed. He would be able to help me. Jesus had apparently made his way into my psyche despite my essentially secular upbringing.

Eleanor got to hear a lot about my vocational cluelessness as well as my difficulties with spiritual practice. After returning to Boulder, I had fallen into a job as an assistant teacher at a preschool affiliated with Boulder's Buddhist community. It was stressful and exhausting work, but as Brian noticed, the two-year-olds brought out a compassionate part of me that had been largely dormant for several years while I had been so preoccupied with my own pain and struggles. After a series of other miscellaneous jobs, including working at a bookstore and at the public library and doing freelance proofreading for two academic publishers, I decided to give graduate school one last try.

I realized that what I'd actually been interested in all along was theology, not philosophy or religious studies, and I wanted to study Christianity in depth.

In 1993, Brian and I moved to Atlanta so that I could start a master's degree program in theology at Emory University's Candler School of Theology and so that Brian could work on some writing he'd been wanting to do, with the help of an old friend and mentor of his who was now teaching at Candler. For me, the master's program functioned as Sunday school or catechism. I didn't know whether this schooling would relate to a future career, but I knew very little about Christianity and wanted to learn. I was also sporadically attending Catholic Mass with Brian, and we were going to Tuesday-night graduate student dinners at Emory's Catholic Center. Eventually, I started thinking about whether it was time for me to make a formal commitment to Christianity.

At Easter Mass in the Emory chapel in 1995, I had a little religious and vocational epiphany. It hit me: "Oh dear, I think I want to be a Catholic priest." I knew, of course, that the Catholic priesthood wasn't likely to be a possibility for me anytime soon. I told a Catholic friend that I figured women wouldn't be ordained in the Catholic Church in my lifetime unless aliens invaded the Vatican. She thought the issue was, rather, that the aliens needed to *leave* the Vatican.

Since the Catholic priesthood wasn't an option, it seemed that the obvious thing for me to do was to consider the Episcopal priesthood. So I tried being Episcopalian. I started worshiping at an Episcopal church, attending its confirmation class, and talking with Emory's Episcopal chaplain. But somehow it didn't quite click. Then I tried the Methodist Church. I was attending a United Methodist seminary, after all, and had already met many of the requirements for Methodist ordination. I felt comfortable with Methodists, and I liked the theology of Methodism's founder, John Wesley, especially the way he juggles an uncompromising belief in salvation by God's grace alone with an equally uncompromising insistence on the importance of Christian practices like worship, prayer, and charity. But the Methodist Church didn't quite feel like the right place for me either.

These excursions made it even clearer that Catholicism was where I felt at home. How I ended up with Catholic sensibilities I'm not exactly sure. Certainly, an important part of my attraction to Catholicism is my strong connection to monasticism and contemplative practice. I also like the high liturgy of Catholicism—the ritual, the "smells and bells." My husband, my best friend from college, a guy I had a crush on in junior high and high school, my first boyfriend, and even my Zen teacher all had been raised Catholic. For some reason, I seem to be drawn to people who were formed by Catholicism. Maybe I inherited my Catholic proclivities from my Mexican grandmother, along with my brown eyes. She spent most of her life trying not to be Mexican, which included not claiming the Catholicism she was born into, but she asked for a Catholic priest when she was on her deathbed.

I finally decided that it was more important to me to be in the religious tradition that felt right than in the career that felt right, so I decided to go ahead and become a lay Catholic rather than an ordained Episcopalian or Methodist.

Brian noticed that I and my friends Laurie and Jennifer, who also became Catholic as adults, entered the church already disgruntled about certain things. As he says, we got baptized and five minutes later said, "OK, I've had it with this!" He finds this amusing and wonders if it's a new phenomenon in Christianity.

The process of becoming a Catholic is an extended one, and I was glad of that. I wanted some time to ease into this commitment and be sure about it. In one of the rites leading up to baptism, during the regular Sunday Mass, the priest asks those preparing for baptism, "What do you ask of God's church?" and our reply is, "Faith." I like that. I wouldn't have been a good candidate for "believer's baptism," as practiced in some denominations. I couldn't confidently say, "I have faith in Jesus Christ as my Lord and Savior, so please admit me to the church," but I could easily say, "I *want* to have faith, so please admit me to the church." Similarly, I like that in the Nicene Creed, which we recite each Sunday, we say, "*We* believe in one God . . ." and all the rest. On the days when I seriously doubt that *I* believe, I can confidently say that *we* believe, letting the church carry me along in her arms.

As a part of the baptismal rite, though, in response to the priest's questions about whether I believed in God, Jesus Christ, and the Holy Spirit, as described in the Apostles' Creed, I would have to answer, "I do." I was worried about this. I didn't know whether I believed, and I didn't want to be crossing my fingers behind my back when I said I did. Did I believe that this mess of a world is good, as God said it is? Did I believe in a power behind creation who cares about me personally? Did I believe in the possibility of the redemption of all the sin and suffering in the world? Did I believe in the meaningfulness of life even in the face of death? Well, no. Christian faith seemed—and still seems—kind of nuts. But I dearly, desperately longed for that faith, and it seemed to me that my only hope for peace and joy in this life lay in that sort of faith. I consulted with a Jesuit friend and another priest I know, and they assured me that my deep longing for faith would allow me to affirm my faith at my baptism in good conscience.

I was baptized and confirmed at the Easter Vigil Mass in 1998.

Around the same time that I decided to become Catholic, I also started to get back into my Zen practice, after a long hiatus. Along with several people from a local Zen center, I helped start and run a Zen meditation group at Emory. And in the fall of 1997, I went back to Zen Mountain Monastery, which I hadn't visited for five years, for a weeklong sesshin. I wanted to do some intensive practice, but it also felt like I was going home to make peace with my past, since I had been so unhappy when I lived there. It was a difficult but good sesshin, and I was pleased to find that the effortful feel of the practice there had been toned down in favor of a more grace-full feeling. I wondered if it was only my perception of the place that had changed, but others confirmed that it was indeed different.

A fairly new spiritual practice for me is prayer. Having decided to formally become a Christian, I realized that although I had done intensive spiritual practice in the Zen tradition, which bears strong resemblances to certain elements of the Christian contemplative tradition, I had very little experience with the basic Christian spiritual practice of verbal prayer. I said all the communal prayers that are part of the Mass, but I had trouble praying on my own. I had a lot of inhibitions and questions about prayer. So during my last semester at Candler, I arranged an independent study with a similarly prayer-impaired friend and a professor, and we read a bunch of books on verbal prayer, some of which were a big help in getting me over my blocks to praying.

In particular, Karl Rahner, one of the great Christian theologians of the twentieth century, assured me that no matter the depth of my doubts about God and Christianity, I could still pray. "If you think your heart cannot pray," he says, "then pray with your mouth, kneel down, fold your hands, speak loudly, even if it all seems like a lie to you (it is only the desperate self-defense of your unbelief before its death, which is already sealed): 'I believe, help my unbelief; I am powerless, blind, dead, but you are mighty, light, and life and have conquered me long ago with the deadly impotence of your Son.'" This was liberating. Although I couldn't will my heart to have a stronger faith, I could certainly will my body to take a posture of prayer and my mouth to say some words of prayer. Rahner assured me that not only was there no hypocrisy in this, but it was vital that I express my half a mustard seed of faith in this way.

My favorite definition of prayer also comes from Karl Rahner, who says that prayer is opening our hearts to God. In the most familiar type of prayer, verbal or discursive prayer, we open our hearts to God using words. We talk to God, either aloud or mentally. But that's not the only way to pray. Christianity also has a tradition of contemplative prayer, in which we open our hearts to God without words or with very few words. We heed God's call in Psalm 46: "Be still, and know that I am God."

In recent decades, some Christians have been dusting off the Christian contemplative practices and popularizing them. One popular form of contemplative prayer is centering prayer, a practice that comes from the medieval mystical tradition, especially *The Cloud of Unknowing.* Centering prayer is a practice of sitting silently in simple openness to God's presence and God's will and in the longing to know God more fully. Since the mind is prone to wander, you choose a "sacred word" to help bring you back to stillness with God—a word like *God, Jesus, love,* or *mercy.* When you become aware of thoughts, you return gently to the sacred word, a symbol of your intention to rest in openness to God. (The list of recommended resources at the end of the book includes resources on Christian contemplative practice, in case you're interested in exploring this.)

Gerald May, whose writing on willingness and willfulness had been so helpful to me, is one of the founders and leaders of the Shalem Institute for Spiritual Formation, an ecumenical center in Maryland supporting Christian contemplative practice. My husband, Brian, participated in Shalem's Group Leaders Program, which provides training for the leadership of Christian contemplative prayer groups, and a few years later, I participated in the same program. One of the requirements of the program was to lead a seven-session contemplative prayer group, but I got permission, instead, to lead a Zen meditation group especially for Christians.

Another requirement of the Shalem program was to meet regularly with a spiritual director. I hadn't had a spiritual director since Brian and I left Colorado, and this prompted me to seek one out. A few years earlier, I had done a silent weekend retreat with a group of other students from Candler School of Theology at a tiny ecumenical Christian retreat center in rural Georgia called Green Bough House of Prayer. I had met with the spiritual director there and liked her, and I decided it was worth driving three hours each way whenever I wanted to meet for spiritual direction. So I started making regular retreats at Green Bough, and Brian came along too.

After my first visit to Green Bough, I told Brian that it's like a Jesuit retreat center run by your grandma. It has that same palpable sense of being a place of silence and prayer, but it feels softer and homier. There are knickknacks and needlepoint pillows around, and meals are eaten at the kitchen table. Green Bough has two permanent residents, who are living a sort of monastic life—Fay, who offers spiritual direction, and Steve, an ordained minister in the United Methodist Church, who leads the services—and they have room for about ten guests. There is a regular schedule of prayer, based on the Liturgy of the Hours. Each service is centered on reciting psalms and other prayers and also includes periods of silence. Many of the meals are eaten in silence. For a couple of years, Brian and I went on a retreat at Green Bough every month or two.

Partway through my master's program, I had started working for Candler's Youth Theology Institute, which runs a summer theology academy for high school students, and I continued working there after I finished my degree. I was the assistant director, which meant basically that I was the office manager, and I also taught a bit of Zen meditation and Christian contemplative prayer during the summer academies.

At age thirty-three, I still didn't know what I wanted to be when I grew up, but I was sick of being an administrator and decided I had to do something else. I had discovered that what I like best is teaching religion and writing about religion, and even though, several times before, I had considered and dismissed the idea of getting a Ph.D. in religion, I finally decided that that was what I wanted to do. I am now a doctoral student at Emory, focusing on Buddhism and Christianity in the United States and especially on spiritual practices in those traditions. On the side, I teach adult education classes and Sunday school classes and lead workshops, mainly on Zen and also on Christian spiritual practices.

Brian is now on the faculty at Candler, and he had a leave coming up for the 2001–02 academic year. I decided to take a leave from my doctoral program for the spring semester, and we spent the first half of 2002 living at Green Bough House of Prayer. It was after we had already planned our leave that I decided to write *Zen for Christians,* but this worked out perfectly. I used my time off from school to do most of the work on this book, while living in a community centered in prayer.

I sometimes pray about my Zen practice, as I would pray about anything else in my life. I pray about the Zen classes I teach—that God may work through and in me and the class members. And I have prayed, in writing this book, that God may work through my writing to speak a word of truth, of grace, of love.

Practice

Walking Meditation

At a Zen center or monastery, when you sit two or more periods of zazen in a row, the periods of sitting meditation are separated by brief periods of walking meditation, or *kinhin*.

Kinhin serves at least two important purposes. First, it
gives you a chance to stretch your legs and move around
between sitting periods. Second, it is a way to take the awareness being developed in zazen—in still, silent sitting—and
extend it into a slightly more complicated activity: walking.
The movements of the body, the changing scenery as you walk,
the sounds of walking, and so forth, can stir up more thoughts,
so it can be more challenging in walking meditation than in sitting meditation to notice thoughts and return the attention to
the present moment.

The spine and head are held upright, as in zazen. The
gaze is lowered, though not unfocused. A special hand position
is used. Make a fist with your left hand, with the fingers
wrapped around the thumb. Put the fist up against your body,

about at the waist, with the thumb pointing down, and cover the front of the fist with your right hand. Let your elbows fall naturally at your sides. Zen master Shunryu Suzuki says of this hand position that "you feel as if you have some round pillar in your grasp—a big round temple pillar—so you cannot be slumped or tilted to the side."

Kinhin is traditionally done clockwise around the room. In the Soto sect of Zen, you take one small step with each full cycle of the breath, moving continuously but very slowly. In the Rinzai sect of Zen, you walk briskly. If you're doing walking meditation on your own in a small space, you'll probably want to walk slowly.

In zazen, you notice your breathing and your thoughts; in kinhin, you notice your walking and your thoughts. Feel the physical sensations of walking. Feel your feet on the floor. Feel the movement of your legs. Feel your clothing brush against your legs. Feel the sensations as you lift one foot, move it forward, put it down, and shift your weight to it. When you realize that you are no longer attending to the walking, notice the thought and gently return your attention to the walking.

You can do walking meditation anytime you're walking. You need not walk in clockwise circles or put your hands in any special position. Just notice your thoughts and return your attention to the walking, over and over and over. And if you're walking near traffic, raise your gaze!

The Essentials of Walking Meditation

- As you walk, be aware of the physical sensations of each step.
- When you realize that your attention has wandered away from the walking, notice the thought and gently return your attention to the walking.

Notice the thought,
  return to the walking,
    notice the thought,
      return to the walking,
        notice the thought,
          return to the walking, . . .

2

The Buddhist Way of Liberation from Suffering

The Story of the Buddha

Siddhartha Gautama, who would come to be called the Buddha, meaning the Awakened One or the Enlightened One, was born five or six centuries before Christ, into a noble family in a part of northern India that is now Nepal. Siddhartha's father, Suddhodana, was the head of the Shakya clan, so the Buddha is also known as Shakyamuni, "the sage of the Shakyas."

When Siddhartha was conceived—so the story goes—his mother Maya dreamed that a white elephant entered her right side, signifying that her son would have an auspicious life. It was foretold that Siddhartha would either remain at home and become a great emperor or leave and become a wandering ascetic and a great religious teacher. Maya died a week after giving birth, and Siddhartha was raised by Maya's sister, who became

Suddhodana's second wife and later the founder of the first order of Buddhist nuns.

Suddhodana wanted Siddhartha to stay at home to become a great emperor, so Suddhodana gave his son a life of luxury and protected him from all unpleasantness, disease, decay, and death. Siddhartha spent his time in his three palaces—one for the hot season, one for the cool season, and one for the rainy season. He wore fine clothes, ate delicious food, and had musicians to entertain him and attendants to serve him. No one who was sick or old or ugly was allowed near Siddhartha, and even dead flowers were removed from his presence. At age sixteen, he married the beautiful Yashodhara, daughter of a neighboring ruler, and when he was twenty-nine, they had a son, Rahula.

Eventually, Siddhartha got bored and restless with his sheltered, pampered life, and he arranged to take a chariot ride outside the palace grounds. His father made sure that everything along the route would be clean and beautiful and that Siddhartha would only see happy, healthy, young people on his ride.

But as it happened, Siddhartha saw a stooped, gray-haired man with wrinkled skin. He asked his charioteer, Channa, about this strange sight. Channa told him that the man was old. Siddhartha asked if this was the only person who was "old" or if there were others like this. Channa replied that everyone who lived long enough would grow old. Siddhartha was shocked and ordered Channa to take him back to the palace immediately, where he sat by himself brooding about this vision of old age.

On a second trip outside the palace, Siddhartha saw someone who was coughing and shaking and moaning. He asked Channa about this, and Channa explained that this person was ill and that all people are subject to illness. Once again, Siddhartha was shocked and returned to the palace and brooded about this vision.

On a third trip outside the palace, Siddhartha saw a group of sad people carrying a corpse. Siddhartha asked Channa why the man was so still and where they were taking him. Channa explained that the man was dead and that his body was being taken to the cremation ground to be burned. Siddhartha asked if it was unusual for people to die like this, and Channa told him that everyone, without exception, would eventually die. Siddhartha was horrified and confused. How could people just go about their daily lives knowing about the inevitability of suffering and death?

Siddhartha was inconsolable. Nothing would lift his spirits or distract him from his visions of aging, illness, and death. He no longer found pleasure in the delights of the palace, knowing how quickly all things change and that death awaits us all. He saw everything permeated with suffering and impermanence.

Siddhartha took a fourth trip outside the palace and encountered one of the religious wanderers of the time, with a shaved head, a saffron robe, and a look of deep calm and peace. After this fourth vision, Siddhartha knew that he had found his own true purpose.

He returned to the palace and told his father that he wished to leave. His father refused to let him go, but

Siddhartha was determined. In the middle of the night, he took one last look at his sleeping wife and infant son, escaped the palace, and went into the forests in search of a spiritual teacher.

Siddhartha mastered sophisticated meditation techniques with two teachers and then engaged in extreme ascetic practices intended to reduce attachment to sense pleasures. He practiced exercises in breath control, which, rather than leading to liberation from suffering, mainly led to terrible headaches, and he reduced his food intake to a spoonful of bean soup a day, which left him emaciated.

After six years of these austerities, the problems of aging, illness, and death remained unresolved, and Siddhartha decided that the best course was a "middle way" between the self-indulgence of the palace and the self-mortification he had been practicing in the forest. He began to take food to strengthen his body, thus scandalizing his companions in asceticism and leading his later teachings to be known as the Middle Way. He remembered that once, as a child, while sitting under a tree, he had spontaneously entered a meditative state of calm attention, beyond involvement in sense pleasures. He now saw that this was the path of awakening.

Siddhartha went off alone, sat down under a tree, and resolved to persist in meditation until he had found liberation. Through the night, Siddhartha fended off the assaults and temptations of a powerful demon called Mara, and at the break of dawn, at the age of thirty-five, Siddhartha came to complete awakening and liberation from suffering.

Siddhartha—now the Awakened One, the Buddha—remained under the tree for seven weeks. Although he longed to help all suffering beings, he thought it would be useless to try to communicate his realization. But finally he saw that there were some people who would understand, and he was moved by compassion to begin teaching.

He set out to find his former companions. At first, they spurned him, but then they realized that he had been transformed. They became the Buddha's first disciples and the core of his community, which eventually included monks, nuns, and lay followers. The Buddha spent the rest of his life teaching and moving from place to place, and great numbers of disciples gathered around him. He died at the age of eighty, after eating some spoiled food.

From India, the Buddha's teachings spread across Asia. The Zen school of Buddhism developed in China in the sixth and seventh centuries, incorporating elements of China's indigenous Taoist tradition. From China, Zen spread to Korea, Japan, and Vietnam. Just in the past century or so, Zen and other forms of Buddhism have spread to the West.

By the way, you know that smiling bald guy with the big bare belly whom you often see in Chinese restaurants, stores, and homes? That's not the Buddha. That's a tenth-century Chinese monk called Pu-tai (pronounced "boo-dye"), which means "hemp sack," from his wandering through towns with a beggar's sack on his back. The Japanese call him Hotei ("hoe-tay"), and he is also called the Laughing Buddha. He embodies several Chinese ideals. He loved children, his large belly symbolizes prosperity, and his smile and relaxed pose indicate happiness and equanimity. The Buddha who founded Buddhism is not portrayed as fat, bare-bellied, bald, or laughing. He is portrayed as a man of thin to average build, with stylized hair, and often with a hint of a smile but not with the big grin of the Laughing Buddha.

Shakyamuni Buddha, the Founder of Buddhism.

The Laughing Buddha (Pu-tai, or Hotei),
a Tenth-Century Chinese Monk.

Buddhist Teachings: The Four Noble Truths

Buddhism is a practical tradition. The Buddha saw a problem
and found a solution. The problem is suffering, and Buddhism
offers a way of liberation from suffering. In Zen, the Buddha's
teachings are not understood to be divine revelations or doctrines
to be believed. Rather, they are understood to be observations

about human experience—observations made by a human being, the Buddha, that can be made by any human being.

According to Buddhist tradition, the Four Noble Truths were the Buddha's first teaching after his enlightenment, given to his former companions in asceticism. The Four Noble Truths are a summary of the practical wisdom of Buddhism regarding suffering and liberation from suffering.

The First Noble Truth: Suffering

The First Noble Truth is the truth of *duhkha,* a Sanskrit word that means "suffering" or "dissatisfaction." This is the observation that the ordinary, unenlightened human life is permeated with suffering, that our lives don't completely satisfy us. We suffer all sorts of physical pain and emotional pain. We can't always get what we want, and we often get what we don't want. Life never seems to go exactly the way we'd like it to. Of course, we have happy times, pleasant experiences, but we know they won't last, and this makes us uneasy. All things, pleasant or unpleasant, are impermanent. Nothing stands still. All things are changing, fleeting, destined to end, including our own lives. Life is permeated with pain and impermanence, and in the unenlightened life this leads to duhkha, to suffering or dissatisfaction.

Duhkha is what the young prince Siddhartha experienced in his visions of old age, illness, and death. A powerful experience of duhkha is often what brings people into serious spiritual practice—a debilitating illness, a divorce, the death of a loved one.

Something like the experience of duhkha is what led the narrator of Ecclesiastes to exclaim, "Vanity of vanities! All is vanity." He discovered that all of our chasing after satisfaction is in vain. He tried accumulating herds and flocks, silver and gold. He tried building houses and planting gardens and vineyards. He tried keeping slaves and singers and concubines. But he saw that it was all futile, that "all was vanity and a chasing after wind." Lovers of wealth, he realized, will never be satisfied with their wealth, and when we die, the fruit of our toil is left to those who didn't toil for it. Even acquiring knowledge and wisdom "is but a chasing after wind." The wise die and are forgotten just like the fools. We all come from the dust, and we all will turn to dust again. Reflecting on the futility of seeking satisfaction and on the wickedness and oppression in the world, he says that the dead are more fortunate than the living, but more fortunate still are those who were never born. Much of Ecclesiastes is an expression of the suffering and dissatisfaction of the ordinary human life.

Something akin to duhkha is also what Saint Augustine experienced when one of his dearest friends fell ill and died. Augustine says in his *Confessions* that in his grief, his soul "was a burden, bruised and bleeding," and he found no rest or peace in his usual pleasures—in the company of his friends, in laughter and song, in "the pleasures of love," or even in books and poetry. His mind was filled with thoughts of how death would seize everyone, just as it had seized his friend. Wherever he looked, all he saw was death. Augustine's encounter with the pain and impermanence inherent in life left him "sick and tired of living and yet afraid to die."

Buddhism can sound rather gloomy or pessimistic, having as its first premise the truth of suffering, but there are three more truths to go. The first two are the bad news, and the last two are the good news.

The Second Noble Truth: The Origin of Suffering

The Second Noble Truth is the truth of the origin of duhkha. Buddhism observes that the origin of suffering is *trishna,* or craving.

The Sanskrit word *trishna* was originally rendered in English as "desire," which is misleading. Naturally, we have desires—desires for water, food, shelter, sex, companionship, the desire to be comfortable instead of uncomfortable, to have pleasant experiences and avoid unpleasant experiences, the desire to stay alive. Saying that the origin of suffering is "desire" makes it sound like the ideal human state resembles being severely depressed. But Buddhism is not about eliminating desires. Desire, in itself, is not the problem.

The problem is when simple desire becomes "craving"— that is, when desire is possessive or aggressive, when we feel that our desires *must* be satisfied no matter what, when we believe that our joy in life depends on satisfying these desires and we go frantically chasing after what we crave. But this is a chasing after wind. Our desires are inexhaustible, and continually chasing after them leaves us exhausted, frustrated, and still unsatisfied.

As a sort of elaboration on the diagnosis of craving, Buddhism observes that the origin of suffering is the so-called

Three Poisons: attachment, aversion, and ignorance. We crave pleasant and satisfying experiences, and we react to them with attachment—with greed, clinging, grasping. We crave freedom from unpleasant and unsatisfying experiences, and we react to them with aversion—with hatred, anger, aggression. Our attachments and aversions—our possessiveness and aggressiveness—lead us to act in ways that cause suffering for ourselves and others. As the First Noble Truth observes, life is full of pain, and all things are impermanent. So if true satisfaction can be found, it cannot be based on attaching to pleasure and averting pain. We can never completely succeed at either. True satisfaction is found in noticing and letting go of our struggles with our experience and simply being with the experience—*being* the experience—and responding with wisdom and compassion.

These struggles with our experience—our poisonous reactions of attachment and aversion—are rooted in the third of the Three Poisons, ignorance. This refers to a specific sort of ignorance. We are ignorant of what Buddhism calls no-self, or selflessness.

Our usual way of dealing with life is focused on self-centered attachments and aversions, on the desire for things to be the way we want them to be. We view life from the vantage point of "me": what pleases me and what doesn't please me, what helps me and what harms me, what I approve of and what I disapprove of. We tend to think and behave as if we are separate and distinct entities, completely independent of everyone and everything else. Our lives revolve around the "self," which we think needs to be gratified with pleasure, protected from pain, and above all protected from nonexistence.

But our "self"-centeredness is ill-founded. Buddhism observes that the "self" we're so desperately concerned about is an illusion, a fiction, a construction. Our ultimate nature is no-self, or selflessness. This doesn't mean that we don't really exist or are somehow unreal. Of course we are real. It means that our independent "selfhood" is illusory. Everyone and everything is interconnected and interdependent. The Second Noble Truth observes that the ignorance of our selflessness is the origin of our attachments and aversions, which are in turn the origin of suffering.

The First and Second Noble Truths articulate the bad news of the human condition, the bad news of suffering and its origin. I have always liked that Buddhism begins with the bad news. As observed in *The Hobbit,* "It does not do to leave a live dragon out of your calculations, if you live near him." The dragon of pain and impermanence is not just our neighbor but our roommate, and Buddhism begins by acknowledging the dragon in the living room. We seek out the great wisdom of the world because something is wrong, because we hurt, because our life isn't the way we want it to be. The First Noble Truth meets us where we are. It recognizes the suffering we experience over the stark and frightening facts of life: pain and impermanence. Similarly, I have always liked the centrality of the crucifix in Catholicism—not just the cross, but Christ crucified on the cross—an image of God's participation in the fundamental human experiences of pain and death. Because Buddhism and Christianity recognize so clearly and understand so deeply the bad news of human life, I am able to trust that their good news is not naively optimistic but profoundly hopeful. I am able to trust that they have some wisdom to share about living with a dragon.

The Third Noble Truth: The Cessation of Suffering

Now we come to the good news. The Third Noble Truth is the truth of the cessation of suffering, the observation that liberation from suffering is possible. The Second Noble Truth observes that the origin of suffering is craving, and the Third Noble Truth observes that it is possible to be free of craving and thus free of the suffering it causes. We can be free to live a life of joy and compassion.

If we awaken from the ignorance at the root of suffering—the ignorance of no-self—we are liberated from the tyranny of egoism and thus from the suffering created by ego-centered attachments and aversions. We awaken to joy—a joy not dependent on our circumstances—and we awaken to all-encompassing compassion. We are freed to truly care for others and also for ourselves, instead of being caught up in the possessive and aggressive cravings of the "self." We are freed to be "selfish" for everyone and everything, since there is no one and nothing separate from "me." If you hurt, I hurt, because you and I are not separate. If you rejoice, I rejoice, because egoism isn't getting in the way.

In a word, the good news of Buddhism is selflessness. Buddhism is a way of awakening to no-self, or selflessness, and it is a way of compassion, or selflessness. In awakening to no-self, we are freed for the practice of compassion. In awakening to our selflessness, we are freed for a life of selflessness. Buddhism is not self-help but selflessness-help.

This notion of selflessness is not alien to Christianity. When Paul says, "It is no longer I who live, but it is Christ who lives in me," I hear him describing a similar letting go of "self." When Paul says to the church in Rome that "we, who are many, are one body in Christ, and individually we are members one of another," I hear him speaking of our interconnection and interdependence. The commandment to love your neighbor as yourself is about selfless compassion. I think we generally hear it as an exhortation to love others as ourselves despite our natural inclination to do otherwise, but perhaps we can hear it also as an exhortation to realize that others are not separate from us in the way we usually assume they are—that they are not truly "other"—an insight that will lead us *naturally* to love others as ourselves. As C. S. Lewis says, "If I loved my neighbour as myself, most of the actions which are now my moral duty would flow out of me as spontaneously as song from a lark or fragrance from a flower."

To say that our ultimate nature is selflessness doesn't mean that the whole notion of a self is useless or that we shouldn't use the word *I*. Buddhism observes reality from two perspectives: the absolute and the relative. From the absolute, or ultimate, perspective, the "self" is seen as illusory, as a construction that is empty of inherent, independent existence. But from the relative perspective—the ordinary, everyday, conventional perspective—we see a conventional "self" independent of other people and things. In our regular everyday lives, whether we are enlightened or not, we operate from the relative perspective, in which the "self" is a useful illusion and the word *I* makes sense. To chop a carrot, I need to perceive myself and the carrot and the knife and the cutting board as separate from one another. And yet from the absolute point of view, I and the carrot and the knife and the cutting board are *not* separate. The absolute and the relative are called the two truths, or the two levels of truth. Both are true. (Much of the paradoxical-sounding rhetoric in Zen comes from mixing together the absolute and relative ways of talking about reality.)

An analogy might be helpful here. If we examine a strip of film, we see lots of small, separate, still pictures in a row. This is the "absolute" view of a movie. When we run that film through a projector at the right speed and aim the projector at a screen, we see one large moving picture. This is the "relative" view of the movie. From the relative perspective, calling it a "movie" or a "motion picture" makes sense, even though the motion is ultimately illusory. The movie is both many small still pictures and also one large moving picture.

Both the absolute and the relative are important, but Buddhist teachers tend to emphasize the absolute view because it is so much less familiar than the relative view. When we get a glimpse of the world from the absolute perspective, we begin to realize the illusory quality of "self," and we begin to carry our "selfhood" more lightly. The more fully we realize no-self, the more we are freed from our subjugation to ego-centered attachments and aversions. The "self" may keep on making its possessive and aggressive little demands, but instead of groveling in submission, we can smile in amusement and *decide* how to act. We are freed to live more joyfully and compassionately. We are freed to more fully appreciate the wonder of life, with all its pleasure and pain, its beauty and ugliness, and we are freed to center our lives in the needs of all of reality, including ourselves, instead of in our possessive and aggressive desires.

Note that Buddhism does not try to solve the problem of suffering by saying that pain is illusory or unreal. Pain is real—as we are all well aware—and Buddhism will not try to talk us out of that. There is a story about the eleventh-century Tibetan Buddhist teacher Marpa, who was grieving the death of his eldest son:

> His students went to him and found him in great grief, sobbing and wailing. Shocked, they asked, "Teacher, how can you weep when you have taught us that all is impermanence and illusion?"
>
> "Yes, it is true," he said, "and losing a child is the most painful illusion of all."

We are not liberated *from* pain; we are liberated *within* pain. Buddhist meditation teacher Sylvia Boorstein (who is also, incidentally, a practicing Jew) puts it like this: "Pain is inevitable, but suffering is optional." Suffering is the complication that our egoism constructs around simple pain. To be free of suffering doesn't mean that if you lose a child you won't grieve or if you have a root canal it won't hurt. It means, rather, that we can live this pain-full life freely, fully, beautifully, joyfully, compassionately. We can be free of the egoistic delusions that turn pain into suffering for ourselves and others.

Since the complete cessation of suffering can sound like an awfully remote possibility, Sylvia Boorstein has added her own "Third-and-a-Half Noble Truth": "Suffering is manageable." On the way to complete liberation from suffering, our suffering gets more and more manageable. With practice, pain becomes less scary, difficulties can be borne more gracefully, and egoistic desires become less heavy and serious, lighter and more humorous.

The Third Noble Truth says that liberation from suffering is possible and comes from realizing no-self—not from understanding or believing in no-self but from practicing and directly experiencing no-self. So, then, how do we realize no-self? How do we make it real? The Fourth Noble Truth tells us.

The Fourth Noble Truth: The Path

The Fourth Noble Truth specifies the path to the cessation of suffering, the Eightfold Path. The path is divided into three sections—wisdom, ethical conduct, and meditation—which are called the Three Trainings. Every stage of Buddhist practice includes training in all three, but the practice focuses first on ethical conduct, then on meditation, and finally on wisdom.

The word translated as "right" in each step of the Eightfold Path has a connotation of "complete" or "whole." Each step contributes to completeness and wholeness rather than incompleteness or brokenness. I have also seen the translations "skillful" and "realistic." To follow the Eightfold Path is to live skillfully, to live in accord with reality instead of with our ego-centered delusions about reality.

The Four Noble Truths

---

1. The truth of *duhkha* (suffering or dissatisfaction):
   Life is permeated with pain and impermanence, and in the
   unenlightened life, this leads to suffering.
2. The truth of the origin of *duhkha:*
   The origin of suffering is craving—or more specifically,
   attachment, aversion, and ignorance of no-self.
3. The truth of the cessation of *duhkha:*
   Liberation from suffering is possible.
4. The truth of the path to the cessation of *duhkha:*
   The Eightfold Path leads to liberation from suffering:
   Wisdom:
      1. Right view
      2. Right intention
   Ethical conduct:
      3. Right speech
      4. Right action
      5. Right livelihood
   Meditation:
      6. Right effort
      7. Right mindfulness
      8. Right concentration

Ethical Conduct. The foundation of the Eightfold Path is ethical conduct, which includes the practices of right speech, right
action, and right livelihood. That is, in what we say, what we
do, and how we earn a living, we refrain from harmful and self-
centered conduct and cultivate helpful and selfless conduct. We
try to minimize behavior that causes suffering for ourselves and
others and maximize compassionate behavior.

In the history of Buddhism, various monastic codes and sets of ethical precepts have been developed that prescribe more specifically what ethical conduct consists of. We'll take a look at the Sixteen Precepts of Zen in Chapter Four.

Meditation. To do a thorough and lasting job of cultivating ethical conduct and to enable ethical conduct to flow naturally, we need to uproot the source of our unethical conduct. We need to see and uproot our attachments and aversions so that they won't keep growing new sprouts of suffering. So when we have a foundation of ethical conduct, the emphasis of the practice shifts to meditation, which includes right effort, right mindfulness, and right concentration. Right effort is active, energetic engagement in overcoming unwholesome states of mind and cultivating wholesome states of mind. Right mindfulness is maintaining clear, open awareness of reality, observing the experiences of the present moment, both physical sensations and thoughts. And right concentration is collecting and focusing the mind, resting the attention in one place—on the breathing, for instance. Most of the practices in this book involve both mindfulness and concentration; the last practice, "just sitting," is a practice of pure mindfulness.

As we practice meditation—as we put effort into cultivating mindfulness and concentration—we see the thoughts that preoccupy us, the egoistic attachments and aversions from which suffering arises, and we practice noticing them and letting them go, instead of allowing them to dictate our behavior. We begin to experience reality in a way that is clear instead of cloudy, selfless instead of self-centered.

Wisdom. To do a thorough and lasting job of being free of the attachments and aversions that lead to harmful and self-centered conduct, we need to go one step further and uproot the source of those attachments and aversions. So the emphasis of the practice shifts to wisdom, which includes right view and right intention. Right view is understanding reality as it actually is. This unclouded view is based on understanding the Four Noble Truths and no-self. Right view is a selfless view, seeing the insubstantial nature of "self"—experiencing this directly, not just understanding it intellectually. Seeing through the illusion of "self" uproots the source of attachments and aversions, which are the source of suffering. Right intention is an intention in favor of selfless renunciation, nonaggression, and compassion. Meditation is an antidote to two of the Three Poisons, attachment and aversion, and wisdom is an antidote to the root poison, ignorance.

But you may wonder, if wisdom is what frees us from the root cause of suffering, why not start there instead of focusing first on ethical conduct, then on meditation, and only then on wisdom? It simply doesn't work that way for most of us. Without having first tamed the worst of our harmful and self-centered conduct, we will have little luck sitting still with our own minds in meditation; and without having first developed the practice of meditation, we will have little luck uncovering wisdom. The Eightfold Path has been observed over time to be an effective way of liberation from suffering.

The Poisoned Arrow

A student complained to the Buddha that he ignored such issues as whether the universe is eternal or not eternal, whether the universe is finite or infinite, whether the soul and the body are the same or different, whether the Buddha exists after death or doesn't exist after death, or both exists and doesn't exist, or both doesn't exist and doesn't not-exist. The student had decided that if the Buddha wouldn't either answer these questions or admit that he didn't know the answers, the student would leave the religious order.

The Buddha replied with an analogy. Suppose a man is wounded by a poisoned arrow, and his friends rush him to a doctor. Suppose the man says to the doctor, "Wait! I will not let you remove the arrow until I know who shot me—what his name is, what caste he is from, whether he is tall or short or of medium height, what his skin color is, where he comes from. I will not let you remove the arrow until I know what kind of bow was used to shoot me, what kind of bowstring, what kind of feather is on the arrow, and what the arrowhead is made of." This man will die with these questions unanswered. What he needs is to have the arrow removed as quickly as possible.

Likewise, the student of the Buddha who insists on knowing whether the universe is finite or infinite, and so forth, will die with these questions unanswered by the Buddha. We have been wounded by suffering, and we need immediate treatment. Trying to find the answers to all our metaphysical questions will only distract us from the urgent matter at hand. And whatever the answers are to these questions, we still face illness, old age, and death.

The Buddha is a doctor whose first concern is to heal us, to remove the poisoned arrow. The First Noble Truth names the symptom from which we seek relief: suffering or dissatisfaction. The Second Noble Truth diagnoses the cause of this symptom: craving. The Third Noble Truth offers the encouraging prognosis that we can be cured of the disease of craving and thus be free of the suffering it causes. And the Fourth Noble Truth prescribes a course of treatment: the Eightfold Path.

Zen and the Four Noble Truths

The Four Noble Truths are part of all forms of Buddhism, but different Buddhist traditions appropriate these teachings in different ways.

Although Zen does talk about the Eightfold Path, the image of spiritual practice as a path doesn't actually work so well for Zen as it does for some other forms of Buddhism. If Zen is a path, it's a peculiar sort of path. On the Zen path, we eventually realize that we don't need to go anywhere and haven't gone anywhere. In Zen, enlightenment is not understood as a journey from *samsara,* the realm of delusion and suffering, to *nirvana,* the realm of enlightenment and liberation, but as a realization that samsara *is* nirvana. Liberation is found right here, right now, in the midst of this life of pain and impermanence. We practice the Eightfold Path of ethical conduct, meditation, and wisdom not as a way to get to buddhahood but simply because that's what buddhas do. We are expressing our innate buddha-nature. Zen is not a way *to* liberation but a way *of* liberation—a way that manifests our inherent liberation.

I discovered another peculiarity of the Zen appropriation of the Four Noble Truths when I was preparing to teach an adult Sunday school class on Zen and Christianity. I pulled a bunch of Buddhist books off my shelves to see how different authors present the Four Noble Truths, and I found a variety of presentations in textbooks on Buddhism and in books by teachers in Buddhist traditions other than Zen, but I found not a single systematic presentation of the Four Noble Truths in my shelf-and-a-half of Zen books. This isn't actually surprising, given Zen's thoroughgoing and uncompromising focus on practice and experience as opposed to ideas. Zen teachers do regularly allude to the Four Noble Truths, apparently assuming that Zen students are familiar with them from their own reading, but in Zen, even the Buddhist teachings are seen as potential diversions from the removal of the poisoned arrow of suffering.

The heart of the Zen way of liberation is not learning or understanding or believing but practice and experience.

Practice

Noticing Thoughts

Zen meditation is often misunderstood as a practice of stopping thoughts or having no thoughts, but it's actually a practice of noticing thoughts. Zen is not about eliminating thoughts but illuminating them.

Thoughts Are Not Distractions

If you try the practice of counting the breath for even five minutes, you'll probably notice something a little disconcerting: our minds are usually full of noise. It feels like someone left a TV on in there, with the volume way up. And the radio is on too, and the phone is ringing, and the dog next door is barking.

It's easy to assume that all the busy little thoughts scampering about in our minds and capturing our attention are distractions from meditation. But they're not. In fact, *distractions* is precisely the wrong word. *Distractions* implies that all those ideas, emotions, images, plans, memories, fantasies, judgments, and so on, that arise during meditation practice are somehow *other* than practice, that they distract us from what we're "supposed" to be doing. But thoughts are not distractions from practice, interruptions to practice, a hindrance to practice, or an indication of poor practice.

Thoughts are an intrinsic part of Zen practice. They're the fodder for practice. We bring compassionate awareness to the physical sensations of breathing or walking, and we bring compassionate awareness to the thoughts that carry our attention away from the breathing or walking. We notice our wandering thoughts and gently return our attention to the present moment, over and over and over.

People sometimes think, "I can't meditate. My mind is too busy." But your mind isn't too busy. All those thoughts are just stuff to notice, and Zen practice is about noticing.

There's no need to repress thoughts or ignore them. There's no need to judge them or scold them. Simply notice the thoughts. Be aware of them. And if you find yourself repressing, ignoring, judging, or scolding your thoughts, there's no need to repress, ignore, judge, or scold *that*. Simply notice it and return your attention to the breathing or the walking. Whatever arises, notice it and return your attention to the physical sensations of the present moment.

Once while I was living at the Zen monastery, I had a dream that I had put a boom box on the floor in the middle of the empty meditation hall and was blasting Led Zeppelin. I realized that I had been repressing emotions in my Zen practice, and some part of me knew better. Emotions are fine. They are not distractions. Let them arise, notice them, and return to the present moment.

Some thoughts are more insistent than others. Sometimes you notice a thought and let it go and it pops right up again and keeps popping up over and over. It may be that this thought needs some special attention after the meditation period is over. It may point to something you need to take care of. There was a long stretch when, in my zazen, I kept having thoughts about how much I hated my job. I finally realized that I didn't need to just keep noticing and letting go of these thoughts; I needed to get a new job!

Sometimes in zazen, you may experience odd little hallucinations, known as *makyo*. They are often visual—for instance, the light seems to dim or images appear in the surface in front of you—but they can involve any of the senses. Makyo are just another type of thought and are treated like any other thought: notice it and return to the present moment.

The thirteenth-century Japanese Zen master Dogen Zenji said:

To study the Buddha Way is to study the self.
To study the self is to forget the self.
To forget the self is to be enlightened by the ten thousand things.

To realize our inherent selflessness, we study the self. We carefully observe what our minds are up to. We notice our attachments and aversions, our possessiveness and aggressiveness. All those thoughts we get caught up in are not distractions from our Zen practice. They are the activity that we call "self." To observe this self is to be free from its domination and to be enlightened by "the ten thousand things," which means everything.

Noticing Thoughts Compassionately

But what exactly does it mean to "notice" a thought before you return to the breathing or walking?

When I started Zen practice, I tended to stomp on my thoughts or whack them away like hockey pucks, or else I'd try to ignore them or pretend they were never there. But that's not what zazen is about. To notice a thought simply means to bring a moment of attention to it before you return your attention to the physical sensations of the present moment. Know what the thought was. Hear an echo of it. Take a flash picture of it. There may have been a five-minute-long sequence of thoughts that captured your attention, so just notice the last one, the one you were involved with when you realized you were thinking. Don't analyze the thought or elaborate on the thought or think about the thought. Just bring your awareness to it momentarily. Then let it go and gently return your attention to the breathing or walking.

The noticing in Zen practice is precise but also gentle. You notice the thoughts and physical sensations with precision—seeing exactly what's happening with a kind of scientific attentiveness. But this precision is not harsh or critical. You notice the thoughts and physical sensations with gentleness also—with kindness, tenderness, compassion.

Here's a helpful image I learned from a meditation instructor. You're at a train station. Your train is leaving in two minutes. You're weaving through all the people and you run into a friend you haven't seen in a long time. You stop and smile and say a few words and maybe give your friend a hug. Maybe you encourage your friend to give you a call soon. And then you run off to get your train. You don't ignore your friend. You don't run by as if you didn't notice your friend. But neither do you get into a long conversation and miss your train. You stop for just a moment to be with your friend in a warm and genuine way, and then you move on. You don't need to make your friend go away; you just let your friend be, while you run off to get your train.

Treat the thoughts that arise in meditation like that friend at the train station. When you notice that a thought has carried you away from the physical sensations of the breathing or the walking, be with the thought for a brief moment. Don't ignore it or run by without making real contact, but don't get into a long conversation with it either. Stop for a moment to bring compassionate awareness to the thought, and then let it go. (It'll probably give you a call later.) You don't need to make the thought go away; just let it be, and return your attention to the breathing or walking. Hug each thought goodbye and return to the present moment.

Listing Thoughts

The format of my Zen meditation groups for Christians is based on the format of the Christian contemplative prayer groups led by the Shalem Institute for Spiritual Formation. Part of the Shalem format is written reflection following the prayer time, so I decided to try including written reflection in my Zen groups. Even though Zen is so deliberately nonverbal and nonconceptual, I thought it was worth experimenting with written reflection, and I've found it to be helpful, especially the exercise of listing thoughts. I invite the participants in my meditation groups to list all the thoughts they can remember that arose during the meditation time. This exercise helps reinforce the point that thoughts are an intrinsic part of the practice, and writing the thoughts down can help us see more clearly what we are preoccupied with, precisely what our own attachments and aversions are.

You might want to try this now and then. Immediately after a meditation period, jot down as many thoughts as you can remember from the meditation period—every bit of mental activity. If it seems like it was one big blur of thoughts, just try to pull out a few vague shreds of ideas, emotions, images, or whatever.

This list is for no one's eyes but yours, and you can discard the piece of paper or delete the computer file as soon as you've finished, so there's no need for censorship. Include the lustful thoughts, the angry thoughts, the frivolous thoughts, the bored thoughts, the anxious thoughts, the surreal thoughts, the thoughts about the practice—everything.

There is no moral value, good or bad, to the thoughts that simply pop into consciousness. When Jesus says that if you look at someone with lust, you have already committed adultery in your heart, I understand "looking with lust" to mean intentionally entertaining a lustful thought—indulging the thought, savoring it, elaborating on it, spinning fantasies from it—not simply having a lustful thought appear in consciousness. Paul says to the Ephesians, "Be angry but do not sin." Angry feelings in themselves are not sinful. It's what we do with the angry feelings that can be sinful.

As we quickly discover in meditation practice, thoughts arise without our control or consent. I like what Trappist monk Thomas Merton says about this: "Sometimes pious men and women torture themselves at meditation because they imagine they are 'consenting' to the phantasms of a lewd and somewhat idiotic burlesque that is being fabricated in their imagination without their being able to do a thing to stop it." But as Merton also says, "There is no real danger in these things." Morality becomes an issue if we intentionally entertain a thought or, of course, if we act on a thought; but there's nothing moral or immoral about simply having a thought. So feel free to notice *all* of your thoughts, whether naughty, nice, or neither.

3

Zen Teachings and Christian Teachings

Zen Teachings Are Not Doctrines

One night, to entertain myself, I was looking up the names of old friends on the Web to see if I could find out what had become of them, and then I looked up my own name, curious about what I'd find. The search turned up a couple of things I'd written, a bunch of sites mentioning a golfer who happens to share my name, the site of Boykin's Desert Surf Shop (no relation), and an article on Zen and Christianity that I didn't write. I thought this was a weird coincidence—that there was another Kim Boykin involved with Zen and Christianity—but she turned out to be me.

I had given a lecture on Zen to an assembly of the high school students at a Christian school in Atlanta, as part of their "International Awareness Week," which focused on East Asia that year. One of the teachers who had attended the lecture wrote an essay in response, "The Zen of Confusion," which he posted on a Christian Web site. In the essay, he argued that one could not practice Zen as a Christian, despite what I had said, because there are fundamental contradictions between the two traditions. One example he gave was that Christianity teaches that human beings are distinct from God and from each other, but Buddhism teaches that "all is one."

I realized that his argument was based on a misunderstanding of Zen. I had probably not made it clear enough in my lecture that Zen teachings cannot be considered doctrines, beliefs, articles of faith, or the like, in the way that these are often understood in Christianity. As I see it, there are three main types of Zen teachings, none of which are doctrines.

First, some of the teachings of Zen are practical instructions about meditation and ethical conduct, like "Sit on the front half of the zafu" and "Do not misuse sexuality." These are rules, guidelines, advice—teachings about how to practice, how to live, not about what to believe. What happens at Zen centers and monasteries is often called Zen training, and the phrase is apt. Teaching Zen is more like training or coaching than like catechesis or indoctrination.

Second, Zen teachings also include hundreds of *koans,* which are used as a focus for meditation and as a jumping-off point for the Zen master's talks to students. A koan (pronounced "*koh*-ahn") is usually a brief anecdote from Zen's early history in China, often about an interaction between a Zen student and a Zen master or between two masters. Later Zen masters compiled collections of koans, adding to each koan their own commentary and sometimes a verse.

This is a koan from a collection called the *Mumonkan,* or *The Gateless Barrier,* compiled by Mumon, a thirteenth-century Chinese Zen master:

> Shuzan held out his short staff and said: "If you call this a short staff, you oppose its reality. If you do not call it a short staff, you ignore the fact. Now what do you wish to call this?"

> *Mumon's comment:* If you call this a short staff, you oppose its reality. If you do not call it a short staff, you ignore the fact. It cannot be expressed with words and it cannot be expressed without words. Now say quickly what it is.

> *Holding out the short staff,*
> *He gave an order of life or death.*
> *Positive and negative interwoven,*
> *Even Buddhas and patriarchs cannot*
>   *escape this attack.*

Don't get it? Neither do I. Koans are meant to help Zen students awaken to wisdom and compassion, but there is nothing in them that Zen students are expected to believe or really even to understand in any rational or intellectual sense. Many koans seem more understandable if you're familiar with the images and metaphors commonly used in Zen and if you've read the translator's footnotes about the Chinese context and so forth, but even then, koans don't "make sense." Koans are not about words or ideas but about experience. To answer a koan is not to figure it out and come up with a response that is sensible, clever, or even wise but to respond to the koan from a certain state of mind—an awakened state. While koans are a form of Zen teaching, and koan collections are an important and voluminous part of the literature of Zen, koans clearly cannot be understood as "doctrinal."

These first two categories of Zen teachings—practical instructions and koans—are not likely to be misunderstood as doctrines, but some Zen teachings lend themselves more easily to this misunderstanding. I will lump these together in my third category of Zen teachings: those that can sound like doctrines. Teachings like the Four Noble Truths and no-self can sound like statements of truth about objective realities. They can sound like propositions that Zen practitioners are expected to believe. Actually, though, these teachings are observations about human experience, and Zen practitioners are meant to use them as a guide for their own practice and experience.

The First Noble Truth, for instance, is not a proposition about an objective reality but an observation about human experience: that the ordinary human life is permeated by the experience of suffering. Likewise, the Second Noble Truth, that craving is the origin of suffering, is an observation about human experience. We can experience for ourselves how our cravings enslave us and cause suffering for ourselves and others. We can also experience the liberation from suffering that the Third Noble Truth says is possible.

The Fourth Noble Truth falls into my first category of Zen teachings, practical instructions, since it specifies the way of liberation from suffering, but it is also an observation about experience, like all of Zen's practical instructions. The Eightfold Path has been observed to be a way of liberation from the experience of suffering, just as sitting with one's spine upright has been observed to be conducive to the sustained experience of alertness and attention.

The teaching of no-self is often taken as a metaphysical claim, a proposition about an objective reality, and in some forms of Buddhism, that is indeed how no-self is understood: as a claim that there is no such thing as a self. But in Zen, the teaching of no-self, though it is sometimes discussed as if it were a metaphysical claim, is not finally about the existence or nonexistence of some intangible entity but about our way of being in the world. No-self is simply another observation about experience: that it is possible to be liberated from the constriction of a life centered on "self" and to experience life more freely and joyfully and compassionately.

Related to no-self is *nonduality,* the teaching that the things we ordinarily see as separate and distinct from each other or even as opposites are ultimately not two, not separate and distinct. You and I are not two. Nirvana and samsara are not two. The absolute and the relative are not two. Everything in the universe is ultimately not two. Strictly speaking, nonduality does not mean that "all is one." Nonduality means only that all is not two, period. Nonduality negates twoness but without going on to affirm oneness. All is not two, but all is not one either. So *nondual* can be understood to mean "neither two nor one." Again, in Zen, this is not finally a statement about an objective reality but an expression of human experience.

If you find ideas like "neither two nor one" confusing, that's fine. Since this isn't something that Zen practitioners are expected to believe, it's no big deal if you don't understand it. In fact, one function of the paradoxical language so common in Zen is to emphasize that we can't think our way to enlightenment. Zen teachers will happily speak nonsensically, turn the teachings upside down, or yank them out from under you and land you on your behind if that might help awaken you to your inherent selflessness and freedom, which is what the teachings are pointing to. A common image in Zen is a finger pointing to the moon: the finger of the teachings pointing to the moon of enlightenment. Zen is not about understanding the finger but about seeing the moon.

The lack of doctrines is one of the features of Zen that makes it possible to practice Zen as a Christian—or as a Jew, an atheist, a Buddhist, or whatever. There is nothing in Zen to conflict with whatever beliefs you may have about God and the nature of reality. Whatever your beliefs are, if you suffer, Zen has something to offer: a way of liberation from suffering, a way of being freed to live joyfully and selflessly.

I have been contrasting Zen teachings, understood as observations about experience, with doctrines, Christian or otherwise, understood as propositions about objective reality. This is a useful contrast for explaining what Zen teachings are not, but it isn't actually fair to Christianity. I don't want to imply that the only way, or the best way, to understand Christian doctrines is as propositions to be believed.

A contemporary Christian theologian, George Lindbeck, observes that there are currently three main ways of understanding Christian doctrines.

First, doctrines can be understood as "informative propositions or truth claims about objective realities." I have been using this way of understanding doctrines (and Lindbeck's articulation of it) in order to contrast Zen teachings with doctrines. In this approach, Lindbeck notes, doctrines are understood as similar to the propositions of science or philosophy. If we understand Christian doctrines this way, then, for example, the doctrine that Jesus rose from the dead is taken as a religiously significant claim about a particular person and a particular event in history.

Alternatively, Christian doctrines can be understood as "symbols of inner feelings, attitudes, or existential orientations." This approach highlights the similarities between religion and art. If we understand Christian doctrines this way, then the doctrine that Jesus rose from the dead is taken as a religiously significant expression of the meaningfulness of human life even in the face of our mortality, or the ultimate triumph of life and goodness over death and evil, or our ever-present access to the divine even when it seems absent, or something along those lines. (You'll notice that there's a lot more room for interpretation when doctrines are understood in this way than in the first way. This can be considered a problem or a benefit or both.)

If doctrines are understood in this second way, then Zen teachings are like doctrines in being expressions of "inner" realities rather than claims about "outer" realities. But Zen teachings are different in that they are not generally symbolic (except insofar as all language is symbolic). The First Noble Truth, for example, is not an image or a story or a metaphor that expresses the human experience of suffering but rather a direct statement that life is permeated with suffering.

The previous two understandings can be combined so that Christian doctrines are understood both as propositions about objective realities and as expressions of human experience. (Lindbeck finds this understanding of Christian doctrines especially among "ecumenically inclined" Catholics.) So the doctrine that Jesus rose from the dead is understood to be religiously significant both as a historical claim and also as an expression of human experience.

When the Christian high school teacher, in responding to my lecture on Zen, argued that there are fundamental contradictions between Zen and Christian teachings, he was revealing that I had not gotten across how Zen teachings function. He understood Christian doctrines in one particular way—as propositions about objective realities—and he understood Zen teachings in the same way, which is a misunderstanding. Thus he saw contradictions between competing propositions: Zen propositions versus Christian propositions. But since Zen teachings are not propositions about objective realities, they cannot contradict or even compete with Christian propositions about objective realities. Zen teachings are not doctrines in this sense. Zen teachings are, rather, expressions of human experience.

The rest of this chapter will explore some of the similarities and differences between Zen teachings and Christian teachings—an exploration that can offer new insight into both Zen and Christianity. This is one of the things I like about interfaith dialogue: besides being a way of learning about an unfamiliar tradition, it can also be a way of illuminating a familiar one.

Similarities: Zen and Christianity on the Human Condition

If we understand Christian teachings as, at least in part, expressive of human experience, then we can see some significant similarities between Zen teachings and Christian teachings regarding the human condition.

Things Are a Big Mess, but It's OK Anyway

As I see it, Zen and Christianity share this fundamental insight about human life: things are a big mess, but it's OK anyway. (I am borrowing some language here from Zen teachers Charlotte Joko Beck and Ezra Bayda.)

The Zen "big mess" is expressed in the First Noble Truth, the truth of duhkha, of suffering or dissatisfaction. Suffering is a pervasive part of the unenlightened human life. We suffer from the pain and impermanence inherent in this life. That's the bad news.

But it's OK anyway. The Third Noble Truth observes that liberation from suffering is possible. It is possible to live this pain-full life of impermanence freely, compassionately, joy-fully, without fear, without suffering. Our liberation, our enlightenment, is found right here in this world pervaded by pain and impermanence. Despite the big mess, it's OK. However unenlightened we may feel, we are already buddhas, and we need only awaken to our buddhahood. That's the good news.

Christianity also says that things are a big mess, but it's OK anyway. The Christian "big mess" is our fallenness, our sin-fulness, our alienation from God and opposition to God, our failure to trust in God, our failure to love God, neighbor, and self. We have fallen from a state of grace into sin and mortality. That's the bad news.

But it's OK anyway because salvation and eternal life are offered through Christ. Our gracious and merciful God came down from heaven, became human, to save us—to save *us*—not some flawless, sinless, perfectly loving beings but us actual flesh-and-blood humans who are significantly less than perfect. Strange as it seems, God loves and forgives *sinners*. We need only repent of our sins and put our faith in Christ. That's the good news.

These similarities are summarized in the chart. (If you're not into charts—if you just don't think this way—please feel free to ignore it.)

Note that in both Zen and Christianity, we do not find liberation by escaping this messy world. Our liberation is right here in the midst of the mess. We thought we needed to avoid pain. We thought we needed to become sinless. No wonder we were getting so discouraged. But hallelujah, we had it all wrong! Enlightenment is discovered right here in this world of pain and impermanence. We don't have to *become* buddhas; we already *are* buddhas. Salvation is offered to *sinners.* Enlightenment is better than pain reduction, and salvation is better than sin reduction. We can be free from the suffering that we usually attach to our pain. We can be free from the judgment of our sins.

Please note that I am not trying to equate suffering and sin, or enlightenment and salvation. Clearly, there are important differences. I just want to show what I see as some intriguing parallels between Zen teachings and Christian teachings about the human condition. I also hope that this comparison might help you hear anew the amazing Good News of God's grace.

	The bad news: **Things are a big mess . . .**	The good news: **but it's OK anyway.**
ZEN	*Suffering:* The unenlightened life is permeated with the suffering of pain and impermanence . . .	*Enlightenment:* but liberation from suffering is possible. We are already buddhas.
CHRISTIANITY	*Sin:* Humanity has fallen into sin and mortality . . .	*Salvation:* but salvation and eternal life are offered in Christ, through God's grace. God loves sinners.

The Fruits of Liberation and the Role of Effort

But what about reducing the amount of pain or sin in our own lives and in the world? What about selfless compassion for all sentient beings? What about love of God and neighbor? These are obviously good and important things, so where do they fit in?

At least some strains of Buddhism and Christianity say that these good and important things flow out of our liberation. We commonly make the mistake of thinking that practicing in accordance with the values of our tradition will help us attain liberation. But no, we've got that backward. Spiritual practice and love and compassion do not *earn* us liberation; rather, they are the *fruits* of our liberation. A good tree bears good fruit. This is another similarity between Zen and Christian observations of human experience.

In Zen, our buddha-nature—that is, our awakened or enlightened nature—is always already present. Practices such as meditation and following the Buddhist precepts are fundamental to Zen, but not because they will help us earn or achieve or create our buddha-nature. Our buddha-nature is always right here, right now. Meditation and following the precepts are expressions and manifestations of our inherent buddha-nature. The practices of Zen can perhaps help us awaken to our inherent enlightenment, help us realize that the enlightenment we've been seeking is already here—and this realization can be transformative. The "actualization" of our buddhahood in our actions in the world flows out of this realization. Increasingly (in the ideal case), we will act with selfless compassion for all sentient beings. Our meditation and our compassionate action do not *earn* us buddhahood; rather, they are the *fruits* of our inherent buddhahood.

Likewise, in Christianity, our salvation, or "justification," is freely offered by God to those who simply turn in repentance and accept God's overflowing love and saving work, accomplished in Jesus Christ, through the Holy Spirit. Christian practices such as prayer, worship, studying the scriptures, and striving to be loving and moral human beings are, of course, central to Christianity. But we cannot, by doing all those good things, earn or achieve or create our justification. The practices of Christianity are ways to express and incarnate the amazing good news of God's love for us. And they can be ways, perhaps, to discover and accept God's gracious and salvific love—and this acceptance can be transformative. Our "sanctification"—that is, our growing saintliness, our growing faith, hope, and love—flow out of our justification. Increasingly (in the ideal case), our actions will manifest love for God, neighbor, and self. Our faith, hope, and love do not *earn* us justification; rather, they are the *fruits* of our justification.

So in one way, human effort is irrelevant. In both Zen and Christianity, liberation cannot be earned or achieved. But this doesn't mean, of course, that human effort is irrelevant to the religious life. Even though our efforts cannot help us earn or achieve salvation or enlightenment, they might help us open to the realization of our inherent enlightenment or to the acceptance of God's free offer of salvation. Our efforts also play an important role in our more fully manifesting that liberation in the world. We can more fully actualize our enlightenment through compassion for all beings. We can more fully manifest our salvation through love of God and neighbor. More and more, we can live with the love and compassion that are fruits of liberation.

Illusory Differences

There are some purported differences between Zen teachings and Christian teachings that I think are not, in fact, differences.

"Works Righteousness"

When I speak to Christian audiences about Zen as a practice and as a way to liberation, some people get suspicious, thinking that Zen sounds like a Buddhist equivalent of what some Christians call "works righteousness." That is, they suspect that Zen practitioners are trying to work their way to liberation rather than relying on grace, as Christians do.

But this is a misunderstanding of Zen. As we've just seen, Zen practice, like Christian practice, is not about achieving or earning or working toward liberation. In Christianity, we do not work toward salvation. Rather, we simply accept the salvation that our loving and gracious God has freely been offering us through Christ all along. In Zen, we do not work toward enlightenment. Rather, we simply realize that the enlightenment we've been searching for has been right here all along. Neither accepting God's grace nor realizing our enlightenment is a "work," although we use verbs for them and although it can sometimes seem awfully difficult—like hard work—to finally get to the point of accepting God's grace or realizing our enlightenment. Christians who are exploring Zen need not be concerned that Zen is a Buddhist equivalent of "works righteousness."

Incidentally, a similar confusion happens within Christianity. In the same way that some Christians misunderstand Zen as "works righteousness," some Christians misunderstand Catholic Christianity as "works righteousness." Some people think that while the Protestant tradition teaches salvation by grace, the Catholic tradition teaches salvation by works. This isn't true. The Catholic tradition also teaches salvation by grace. In 1999, the Roman Catholic Church and the Lutheran World Federation signed a "Joint Declaration on the Doctrine of Justification" about this very point. In the declaration, the two traditions confess together that "by grace alone, in faith in Christ's saving work and not because of any merit on our part, we are accepted by God and receive the Holy Spirit, who renews our hearts while equipping and calling us to good works." By grace alone, we are accepted by God. And the Holy Spirit calls us to good works, which are not a cause of justification but its fruits: "We confess together that good works—a Christian life lived in faith, hope and love—follow justification and are its fruits." There are some important differences in the understanding of justification between the Catholic Church and various Protestant denominations and also among Protestant denominations, but on this fundamental point that justification is by grace, there is general agreement.

Optimism and Pessimism

Several years ago, a friend of mine asked me how I reconcile the Christian doctrine of human depravity and the fallen state of the world with the Zen conviction that we are all buddhas. This had never struck me as a problem before, but why not? It certainly *sounds* like a problem. How *do* I reconcile inherent fallenness with inherent buddhahood?

Well, I don't. It doesn't make sense to compare Zen and Christianity by examining inherent fallenness versus inherent buddhahood. Setting it up that way is comparing the "big mess" part of Christianity with the "it's OK" part of Zen. Inherent fallenness is Christianity's bad news, and inherent buddhahood is Zen's good news. Both Zen and Christianity have bad news and good news. Both traditions say that things are a big mess, and both say that it's OK anyway. Comparing the bad news of one with the good news of the other leads us to see supposed differences that are in fact illusory.

I most often hear this mistake from Westerners who are disenchanted with Christianity. They talk about how much more optimistic and life-affirming Buddhism is than Christianity, since Buddhism talks about our inherent buddhahood while Christianity talks about our inherent sinfulness. But this isn't fair. *Of course* Buddhism sounds more optimistic if you compare Buddhism's good news with Christianity's bad news.

When Westerners first encountered Buddhism, they tended to make the opposite mistake. They saw Buddhism as pessimistic because of its first premise, its First Noble Truth of suffering, in contrast with the Good News of Christianity. But again, this isn't a fair contrast. *Of course* Buddhism sounds more pessimistic if you compare Buddhism's bad news with Christianity's good news.

We were discussing the good news and bad news of Zen and Christianity in a session I led of a Methodist Sunday school class for parents of young children. One father commented that Christian parents need to be sure to teach their children the good news of God's grace and not just the bad news of human sinfulness, so that their children won't grow up and feel like they have to leave Christianity to find some good news. I agree. Not being able to find good news in Christianity would be a sad reason to leave the church and a sad comment on one's religious education. I would add, conversely, that if children do not hear what their religion says about the bad news of life, then when they inevitably discover the bad news for themselves, they may think that they have to look elsewhere for a religious or nonreligious worldview that recognizes what a mess human life is. Christianity would be incomplete without both the bad news and the good news, and Zen, too, would be incomplete without both the bad news and the good news.

Real Differences

There are, of course, many real and significant differences between Zen teachings and Christian teachings.

Although it isn't fair to compare the good news of one tradition with the bad news of the other, it *is* fair to compare

Zen's good news with Christianity's good news or Zen's bad news with Christianity's bad news. Even if both traditions say, "Things are a big mess, but it's OK anyway," they have different teachings about what the big mess is and why it's OK anyway.

In Zen, the big mess is suffering, which is rooted in the illusion of "self." In Christianity, the big mess is sin: our alienation from God and the resulting violations of the divinely established order. So in Zen the root problem is faulty perception, while in Christianity the root problem is faulty relationship.

In Zen, "it's OK anyway" because we can awaken to our inherent freedom and selflessness. In Christianity, "it's OK anyway" because salvation is offered through faith in Jesus Christ. There is no God or messiah involved in Zen realization as there is in Christian salvation. Again, the relationship with the divine is central in Christianity.

There is also a significant difference between the role of the Buddha in Zen and the role of Christ in Christianity. In the Zen tradition, the Buddha is not understood to be any sort of god, messiah, savior, or supernatural being, but simply a human being, a great teacher and example, someone who found a way of liberation from suffering and taught this way to others. While the Buddha and Christ are alike in some significant ways—and you can now find many books comparing them and their teachings—in at least this one crucial way they are not alike. They play different roles in the liberation of their followers. The Buddha *shows* the way, while (in most forms of Christianity) Jesus Christ *is* the way. Of course, Jesus' life is also an example for Christians to follow, but it is faith in Christ that is salvific. There is no comparable "faith in the Buddha" in Zen. In Christianity we are saved through Christ, whereas in Zen we are awakened not through the Buddha but rather by following the Buddha's teachings and example. Jesus is necessary for salvation, but the Buddha is not necessary for enlightenment. Zen practitioners are grateful to the Buddha for his teachings, but someone else could have discovered and taught the same things he did. If archaeologists were to find evidence tomorrow that the Buddha never lived, it would have little to no effect on Zen practitioners or Zen practice.

The Buddha's role is more like that of a Christian saint than that of Christ. The Buddha, like a saint, is an example to follow. We can be realized buddhas, and we can be saints. We can also be like Jesus in some respects, but in one fundamental and all-important respect we can never be like Jesus: we cannot be God. Jesus Christ is both fully human and fully divine, and the rest of us are only fully human.

In some ways, Zen and Christianity are not different so much as they are incommensurable. That is, in some ways, Zen and Christianity can't be compared because they aren't even talking about the same things, so comparing them would be like comparing tennis and mathematics, as Thomas Merton said. For instance, you can't compare what Zen and Christianity say about God, since Zen doesn't say anything about a God or gods. Also, Zen does not make statements about the nature of reality that go beyond what can be experienced. There is no divine revelation in Zen, as there is in Christianity. Zen has nothing to say about the origin of the world or about what happens after death, so we can't compare Zen and Christian views about these issues. (Although the Buddhist tradition talks about reincarnation, I have heard little to nothing from Zen teachers or in Zen books about what happens after death.)

In Zen-Christian dialogue, the differences between Zen and Christianity are sometimes minimized or ignored—usually, I think, in a well-meaning attempt to promote harmony and respect among people of the two traditions—but I don't think this minimizing or ignoring is necessary or fruitful. The differences between Christianity and Zen are significant and interesting, and in my opinion, they need not lead to animosity between Christians and Zen practitioners, and they are no hindrance to the practice of Zen by Christians.

Zen and Christianity do also share significant common ground, especially, as we've seen, in their understandings of the experience of being human. Christian theologian David Tracy notes that while the Buddhist and Christian ways are clearly not the same, "neither are we two, in any easy way, merely other to one another." Borrowing the Buddhist notion of nonduality, Tracy suggests that perhaps "we are neither the same nor other, but not-two. Only the further dialogue will tell."

Welcome to the dialogue!

Practice

Zazen: Following the Breath

At many Zen centers and monasteries, beginners are taught the practice of counting the breath. After a while, a student may shift to the practice of counting only the exhalations instead of both the inhalations and exhalations. And then, as counting the breath becomes easier, the student may be given the practice of following the breath, which is like counting the breath but without the counting.

In following the breath, you simply feel the physical sensations of the breathing, and when you realize that your attention has wandered, you notice the thought and return your attention to the breathing. The posture instructions are the same as for counting the breath.

Going from counting the breath to following the breath is like having your training wheels removed. The counting is a support, making it easier to stay with the breath and easier to notice when your mind has wandered off. In following the breath, you're a little more on your own.

Note that breathing is not something you have to *do*. In zazen, just let the breathing happen, and observe it.

Similarly, attending to the present moment is not something you have to *do*. Clear awareness is the environment of our wandering thoughts. When, rather than grabbing on to thoughts or pushing them away, we simply notice them and let them be, clear awareness is revealed.

The Essentials of Following the Breath

- Find a sitting posture that allows you to have an upright spine, and to be stable and completely still.

- Keep your eyes open, with your gaze lowered at about a 45-degree angle, soft-focused, eyelids droopy.

- Take one or two slow, deep breaths. Then let your breath be however it is.

- Let your attention settle in your *hara* (about two inches below the navel).

- Attend to your breathing—to the physical sensations of each breath.

- When you realize that your attention has wandered away from the breathing, notice the thought and gently return your attention to the breathing.

Notice the thought,
  return to the breathing,
    notice the thought,

> *return to the breathing,*
>   *notice the thought,*
>   *return to the breathing, . . .*

Swirling Thoughts and Swirling Snow

When I'm driving, usually I spin around in my thoughts and maybe talk with my husband, Brian, or listen to the radio. But sometimes I need a break from my brain, so I notice my thoughts and return my attention to just driving, notice my thoughts and return to just driving, and so on.

I was doing this once when Brian and I were on the long drive home to Atlanta from his mother's house in Tampa, and I thought of a snow globe—you know, one of those clear globes or domes with water and a little scene inside. You shake the globe to stir up the "snow," and then you set it down and watch the snow fall over the scene.

In our ordinary lives, our thoughts are almost continually swirling around. In Zen practice, we repeatedly set our minds down to let the thoughts settle, by returning our attention to the breath. We notice the swirling thoughts and set our minds down, notice the swirling thoughts and set our minds down, and so on.

The snow will settle if we simply set the snow globe down and let it be. Shaking the snow globe in a certain way in an attempt to make the snow settle more quickly just stirs the snow up more. It's the same with thoughts. All of our attempts to control our thoughts—to force them to settle—just stir them up more. The thoughts will settle on their own if we simply set the mind down, letting our attention return to the breathing.

After I'd played for a while with the snow globe image—which is just a variation on a common image in Zen, of mud settling out of water if you simply let the water be—I decided I wanted to get a snow globe to use when I teach Zen. On another drive home from Tampa, Brian found one in the gift shop connected to a restaurant just off the interstate. It has a picture of palm trees along a Florida beach and sparkly multicolored glitter instead of white "snow," and the great thing is, it was designed so that you can remove the picture and insert your own. On the Web, I found a nice picture of the scowling, wide-eyed face of Bodhidharma, the "first patriarch" of Zen in China, and printed it out, cut it to the right shape, and put it in the snow globe.

The sparkly thoughts swirl around Bodhidharma's head and then settle. I like this. When I'm busy with thoughts, it feels like my energy is all up in my head, and when I notice the thoughts and return to my breathing, I let my energy and my attention settle back down toward my hara. Also, being caught up in thoughts sometimes feels to me like there's a cloud of stuff floating around my head, keeping me from seeing clearly what's going on right here and now besides my own mental chatter. So returning to the breathing feels like letting the thoughts settle out so that they're no longer obscuring my vision.

Note that swirling snow is an intrinsic part of a snow globe. You don't make a better snow globe by freezing it so that the snow can't move or by extracting the snow. Likewise, swirling thoughts are an intrinsic part of Zen practice. We just watch our thoughts, as we watch the snow:

> *Notice the swirling snow,*
>   *set down the snow globe,*
>   *notice the swirling snow,*
>   *set down the snow globe,*
>   *notice the swirling snow,*
>   *set down the snow globe, . . .*

4

Enlightenment: Already and Not Yet

We Are Already Buddhas

If Zen practice seems like a project, like one more item for your already oppressively long "to do" list, it may be that you're misunderstanding what Zen practice is. It's easy to think that Zen is another thing we need to do to get where we want to be, another project to put on top of our already precarious pile of projects. I certainly approach my own Zen practice that way a lot of the time. We tend to think that our new and improved life is off in the future somewhere and that Zen will help us create that life. But Zen is not another project. It isn't even a project to get rid of our projects.

Zen is an unproject, a nonproject. Zen is not about striving to get somewhere else. It's about being right here. Zen is not about being someone else—someone more peaceful and wise, someone happier and more together. It's about being ourselves, exactly as we are right now. Zen is not about becoming a buddha but about realizing our inherent buddhahood. This is the good news of Zen. We already *are* buddhas. Things are OK *right now.*

Several years ago, I was really struggling with my Zen practice and also with my practice of prayer. It was all making me feel kind of crazy. And I thought, "You know, I might be a lot better off if I simply gave up on all this spiritual practice stuff, at least for a while, and just lived my life as it is." I didn't know if I could manage that. Every religious tradition seems to have its own special form of guilt, and I get plagued with Zen guilt if I don't do zazen regularly. But I thought that maybe I could get over that and just leave my life alone.

And then I realized, Hey, wait a minute! That's what Zen practice is all about—practicing being with our actual lives, seeing the freedom and joy that are right here, in our lives just as they are. We don't need to change anything in order to be free. We don't need to wait until we've made further progress on a spiritual "journey." The freedom we're searching for is right here, wherever we are. In zazen, we rest in that freedom. We express that freedom. We manifest our inherent buddhahood.

This doesn't mean that we shouldn't try to change ourselves or our situation or the world. The desire for change can be rooted in selfless compassion for others, for ourselves, for everything. When we open our awareness to things as they are, the wise and compassionate response may be to try to change things. The problem, as the Second Noble Truth observes, is when the desire for change is not just a desire but a craving, when our desire for change is centered on the "self," when it is possessive and aggressive. Craving gives rise to suffering for ourselves and others.

But this sounds a little worrisome. Our desire for change usually *is* possessive and aggressive. Our Zen practice usually *is* motivated by ego-centered desires. That's just fine. Of course we're self-centered. That's inevitable and normal, and that's what we practice with. Our attachments and aversions, our possessiveness and aggressiveness, the self-centered quality of our desire for change—these are fodder for practice. We notice the possessiveness of our desire for change, and we return our attention to the present moment. We notice the aggressiveness of our desire for change, and we return our attention to the present moment. We notice how we're turning Zen into another self-improvement project, and we return our attention to the present moment.

In Zen, we practice opening our compassionate awareness to things exactly as they are, including ourselves exactly as we are, with all our self-centered projects. Zen is not about changing ourselves. It isn't even about changing our desire to change ourselves. We can't change ourselves into buddhas, not even by getting rid of our desire to change ourselves into buddhas. We are already buddhas. Nothing about us needs to be different.

Before he got into Zen, Issan Dorsey did all sorts of drugs, had frequent run-ins with the police, and performed in drag shows in San Francisco's North Beach district, billed as "Tommy Dee, the boy who looks like the girl next door." Once, at a question-and-answer session at the Zen Center where Issan was abbot, a Zen student said to him, "'I've been studying for six months now and I don't notice any difference in my behavior or thoughts. You've been doing zazen for twenty years, have you noticed any difference in yourself?' After a few minutes of hesitation and puzzled facial expressions, Issan replied, 'Well, I don't wear high heels anymore.'"

Although Zen practice may change our behavior or thoughts, that isn't fundamentally what it's about. Zen practice is an expression of our inherent buddhahood. We don't need to change ourselves into buddhas. We are already buddhas.

We Are Not Yet Awakened

While Zen observes that we are already buddhas, Zen also observes that we are not yet awakened. This is not news to us, of course. It is readily apparent that we are not awakened. We may be buddhas, but we sure don't feel like buddhas, and we don't act much like buddhas either. The Third Noble Truth says we can be liberated from suffering, but we aren't liberated yet. We suffer, and we cause suffering for others. This is the bad news of Zen. Our lives are permeated with suffering. We are not yet awakened. And awakening isn't easy. Letting go of the attachments, aversions, and ignorance that give rise to suffering takes practice and determination.

We may begin Zen practice out of simple curiosity, but we are probably hoping that Zen will change our lives in some way. Perhaps we want to lower our blood pressure or improve our concentration. Perhaps we have encountered pain and impermanence in a way that has frightened and confused us, and we are trying to make sense of it all. Perhaps we once had a taste of our inherent selflessness and freedom, but it has faded into a poignant memory and we want to recapture it. Or perhaps we just have a vague feeling that there's more to life than this. In any case, we want something to change. We want our lives to be different. We want our lives to be better. And we sense that spiritual practice is the key.

At the monastery where I lived, each night at the end of evening zazen, while everyone is still sitting silently in the darkened meditation hall, the timekeeper chants:

Let me respectfully remind you,
life and death are of supreme importance.
Time swiftly passes by and opportunity is lost.
Each of us should strive to awaken.
Awaken. Take heed.
Do not squander your life.

Zen master Dogen said that you must practice meditation as if your hair is on fire. If your hair is on fire, what do you do? You put out the fire! You don't procrastinate. You don't give the fire your partial attention while also attending to other things. You don't wait to do something about it until someone else shows up who can help you. If your hair is on fire, you put every bit of your attention and energy into immediately and completely extinguishing the fire. Zen practice requires this same urgent, single-minded intensity.

Bodhidharma and Hui-k'o are models of the intensity and determination needed in Zen. The semihistorical, semilegendary Bodhidharma is known as the first patriarch of Zen in China. Buddhism was already in China when the Buddhist master Bodhidharma arrived from India in the sixth century, but Bodhidharma is credited with bringing to China a form of Buddhism focused on meditation and direct realization—a form of Buddhism that when melded with the indigenous Chinese Taoism would become Zen Buddhism (called Ch'an in Chinese). Bodhidharma reputedly spent nine years at Shao-lin monastery in northern China doing zazen facing a wall. He is always depicted with a big nose and a bushy beard—very un-Chinese—and with huge eyes. I've heard two explanations for the huge eyes. One is that his Indian eyes looked strangely large to the Chinese. The other is that Bodhidharma once got so furious about falling asleep while doing zazen that he cut off his eyelids. Where his eyelids fell to the ground, they grew into the first tea plant, and ever since, tea has kept Zen meditators awake and invigorated.

The Buddhist monk Hui-k'o traveled to Shao-lin monastery to become a student of the great master Bodhidharma. Hui-k'o stood in the snow outside Bodhidharma's cave for several days and nights, repeatedly asking Bodhidharma to teach him, but Bodhidharma ignored him and kept facing the wall. Finally, to prove his earnestness, Hui-k'o cut off his own left arm and presented it to Bodhidharma, who then accepted Hui-k'o as a student. After six years of intensive meditation training with Bodhidharma, the master designated Hui-k'o as his successor, the second patriarch of Zen in China.

Or course, the stories about Bodhidharma and Hui-k'o may well be hyperbolic—one historian says that Hui-k'o's arm was probably cut off by bandits—but the point of the stories is clear. We must practice like someone whose hair is on fire, like someone who would do zazen facing a wall for nine years and cut off his eyelids to stay awake, like someone who would cut off an arm to receive the teachings. We are not yet awakened, and we should strive with all our might to awaken.

Already and Not Yet

But there seems to be a serious contradiction here.

Zen says that we are already buddhas—already "awakened ones"—and Zen also says that we are not yet awakened—not yet buddhas. Zen says that striving won't get us anywhere, and Zen also says that we must strive to awaken. Zen says that we can't work our way to liberation, and yet Zen practice sure does seem like hard work. Zen says that we don't need to change a bit, and yet we're suffering and can be liberated from suffering, and wouldn't it be a tremendous change to be liberated from suffering? Zen says that enlightenment can't be attained, and Zen prods us to enlightenment.

What's the deal? Are we buddhas, or aren't we buddhas? Is striving pointless, or is striving vital? Does Zen practice change us or not? Are we inherently enlightened, or do we need to become enlightened? Are we there yet or aren't we? Which is it?

The answer is *both*. We are already buddhas, and we are not yet buddhas. We are inherently enlightened, and we must strive to become enlightened.

Does this make logical sense? No.

Or the answer is *neither*. Zen teacher Hakuun Yasutani says that when one who is inherently a buddha attains enlightenment and becomes a buddha, it's "like some sort of goblin who puts one head on top of another." But those who say that enlightenment is unnecessary are "like fools who cut off the head and then look for the tongue." He sums it up: "If you're enlightened, it's no good; if you're not enlightened, it's even worse." You can't say you're already a buddha, and you can't say you're not yet a buddha.

Does this make logical sense? No.

In trying to make sense of this, we might assume that the answer is really a combination of *already* and *not yet*—that in one sense of the word *enlightened,* we are already enlightened, and in another sense, we are not yet enlightened. Or we might assume that the answer is really somewhere in between *already* and *not yet*—that we need to find a "middle way" between not striving at all and striving mightily. These answers are satisfyingly rational. But Zen isn't saying these rational things. Zen's answer is nonrational.

When Zen says anything at all, Zen often says one thing and the opposite thing at the same time. Or Zen denies one thing and the opposite thing at the same time. This paradoxical language points to a truth beyond language, beyond logic, beyond purely intellectual understanding.

We are both already enlightened and not yet enlightened. Or we are neither already enlightened nor not yet enlightened. Or both of those. Or neither.

I personally don't much like this sort of paradoxical rhetoric. I think it gets overused in Zen, when some ideas could perfectly well be expressed in ways that are more straightforward and also more helpful to those seeking liberation. I think paradoxical language sometimes gets used in place of addressing hard questions or thinking things through clearly. But I do think there is an important place in Zen for paradoxical language.

Zen master Shunryu Suzuki's *Zen Mind, Beginner's Mind* is a classic of American Zen and is full of paradox. Suzuki says, for instance, "For us, complete perfection is not different from imperfection. The eternal exists because of non-eternal existence." For many years, even while I was living at the Zen monastery, I suspected that a lot of the enthusiasm for this book was an "emperor's new clothes" phenomenon. That is, a few respected people said it was wonderful, so then everybody said it was wonderful. I figured its aura of profundity was largely due to Suzuki's congruence with our image of mountaintop gurus—his short sentences and limited English vocabulary and his paradoxical language that sounds deep even though nobody has a clue what it means. More recently, I've come to think that the emperor really does have clothes and that paradox is the best form of language for expressing some of the fundamental truths of human existence, like the truth that we are already enlightened and not yet enlightened.

Expressions of Already and Not Yet

One way that Zen points to truths beyond logical understanding is with paradox. Zen also uses images, stories, poetry,
actions, silence—whatever works. Here are a few expressions
of "already and not yet."

Yasutani Roshi says that searching for enlightenment is
like riding around on your ox searching for your ox:

"Where are you going on your ox?"

"Oh, yes, I'm going to look for my ox."

"If it's your ox you're looking for, aren't you riding on it?"

"Ah! So I am!"

Realizing that you are already on your ox is enlightenment. "This is a kind of silly thing," Yasutani comments, "but
there is not even one unenlightened person who knows that
sentient beings are originally buddhas." Even the Buddha, until
he became enlightened, had not yet realized that all beings are
already buddhas. Even the Buddha had to awaken to his buddha-
nature.

A more familiar version of the ox story is searching all
over the house for your glasses while you have them on:

"What are you looking for?"

"My glasses."

"Your glasses are on your face."

"Oh. Duh."

Realizing that you already have your glasses on is enlightenment. Nothing has changed—your glasses were already
on—but something important has changed. Now you *know*

your glasses are on. Now you can settle into the comfy chair and read your book. Of course, you could have settled into the comfy chair to read your book before, but you didn't know that. You already had what you needed, but you hadn't yet realized that you had what you needed.

The Japanese Zen master Hakuin offers this verse on liberation from suffering:

The ogre outside shoves the door,
The ogre inside holds it fast.
Dripping sweat from head to tail
Battling for their very lives,
They keep it up throughout the night
Until at last when the dawn appears
Their laughter fills the early light—
They were friends from the first.

We are already friends with the ogre on the other side of the door, but we haven't yet realized it. It isn't necessary to defend ourselves from the ogre or defeat the ogre or scare the ogre away or negotiate with the ogre or make peace with the ogre. We need only recognize the ogre as an old friend. Then we can have a good laugh together and relax and enjoy ourselves.

These "already and not yet" images might actually make a little too much sense. For a while, I thought I had solved the puzzle of "already and not yet." I thought the paradoxical language was a poetic affectation. I thought one could, in fact, make logical sense of the apparently contradictory Zen teachings about enlightenment.

Here's the way I had it figured. Everything about my life is already OK exactly as it is *except* that I haven't realized that yet. That's the only thing about my life that needs to change. That's all I need to strive for: that realization. To be liberated from suffering, I obviously don't need to become rich or famous or powerful. I don't need to become smarter or more attractive. I don't even need to become less depressive or more centered or wiser. All I need is an enlightenment experience. All I need is the realization that everything about my life is OK exactly as it is.

Fortunately, I had that wrong. If that's what Zen says, it wouldn't be such good news. But Zen has some really good news. Everything about my life is already OK exactly as it is, *including* my not having realized that yet. I have not yet awakened, *and* I am already a buddha. The paradoxical rhetoric here is not an affectation. The Zen tradition is pointing to the truth as best it can using the limited tool of language. We are already buddhas, and we are not yet awakened.

Already and Not Yet in Practice

It is said that there are three requirements for Zen practice: great faith, great doubt, and great determination.

Great faith is trusting that things really are OK in some fundamental way, trusting that we are all buddhas. Great faith is believing that the Buddha and all the other enlightened teachers of the past were not lying or deluded but were pointing to the truth when they taught their way of liberation. Great faith knows the "already" of Zen: that we are already buddhas.

Great doubt is the gut-wrenching doubt that things could possibly be OK exactly as they are. It is the doubt, sometimes approaching despair, that this life of pain and impermanence could ever possibly be a life free of suffering and full of joy. Great doubt knows intimately that things are a big mess, that the world is full of suffering and our own lives are full of suffering. Great doubt knows the "not yet" of Zen: that we are not yet awakened. Great doubt even doubts the "yet" in "not yet." That is, great doubt suspects that liberation isn't even possible in such a mess of a world.

And great determination is the determination to awaken, to realize our buddhahood, to be liberated from suffering and to liberate others from suffering, to practice as if our hair is on fire.

We need all three. Great faith, great doubt, and great determination are the legs of the tripod on which our Zen practice stands. Our practice will topple if we're missing one of these legs. If we have faith but no doubt, we may be complacent. If everything is completely OK, why practice? If we have doubt but no faith, we may be driven to despair. If everything is an irredeemable mess, why practice? The dynamic tension between faith and doubt—between the "already" and the "not yet"—gives us a reason to practice. Then we just need the determination to practice.

Already and Not Yet in Christianity

I have borrowed the language of "already" and "not yet" from Christian theology. For the early church, God's reign had *not yet* come. Christians awaited the imminent return of Christ to judge the living and the dead and to inaugurate the kingdom of God on earth. Some Christian theologians in the twentieth century understood God's reign to be here *already,* having made itself known, or having come to be, in Jesus' life, death, and resurrection. Other contemporary Christian theologians have reaffirmed the future nature of God's reign. And others have proposed combinations of "already" and "not yet": that God's reign is in some sense already here and in some sense not yet here.

As far as I know, no Christian theologian has simply asserted both the "already" and the "not yet" with the brazen nonrationality we find in Zen. That is, no one has tried to say that God's reign is both already fully here and also not yet here at all. This strategy might be worth a try, and I don't think it's as radical as it might sound. The Christian tradition long ago settled on some paradoxical language for talking about God and Jesus. God is a Trinity—that is, God is both one and three. Does this make logical sense? No. Jesus Christ is both completely human and completely divine. Does this make logical sense? No. Is it OK that these key pieces of Christian theology don't make logical sense? Yes, at least in the opinion of many strands of Christianity. The Christian tradition is using the limited tool of language to point to truths beyond language.

Compassion: The Manifestation of Enlightenment

The two basic attributes of an enlightened being are wisdom and compassion. So far in this chapter, we've been talking about wisdom—that is, about realization or awakening or enlightenment. But the Zen way of liberation is not only about realizing our buddha-nature but also about manifesting, or "actualizing," that realization in the world. It is not only about realizing our selflessness but also about living selflessly. The fulfillment of the way of Zen is a life of compassionate service in the world.

The ideal type in Zen is the *bodhisattva*. A bodhisattva is usually defined as one who seeks enlightenment but renounces his or her own attainment of complete enlightenment in favor of a compassionate effort to help all beings to enlightenment. Another understanding is that bodhisattvas seek their own complete enlightenment because this is the best way to achieve their primary goal of leading all beings to enlightenment. In either case, the primary concern of the bodhisattva is the liberation of others.

The Sixteen Precepts of Zen describe a life of wisdom and compassion. The first three precepts, called the Three Refuges, relate to the so-called Three Treasures, or Three Jewels, of Buddhism: the Buddha, the Dharma, and the Sangha. The Buddha refers both to the historical Buddha and also, more generally, to our inherent buddha-nature. The Dharma is the teachings of Buddhism. And the Sangha is the community of practitioners. We "take refuge" in the Buddha, the Dharma, and the Sangha. The next three precepts are general ethical guidelines: resolutions to avoid evil, to do good, and to liberate all sentient beings. And the remaining ten precepts are specific guidelines for how to go about avoiding evil, doing good, and liberating all sentient beings. Traditionally, these precepts were only expressed negatively—specifying how *not* to behave—but some contemporary Zen communities have added positive expressions of the precepts—specifying how *to* behave.

The precepts of Zen are a description of how an enlightened person would naturally live, and for those who are not yet fully enlightened—which probably means everyone—the precepts are a prescription for how to behave *as if* we were fully enlightened, how to live in a way that is conducive to our own and others' liberation from suffering. For a fully realized buddha, wise and compassionate action would be natural and spontaneous. For the rest of us, wise and compassionate action may come naturally at times, but at other times it won't, so the tradition has handed down some guidelines to follow for living wisely and compassionately.

I find it interesting that two of the precepts are related to not saying bad things about other people. The twelfth precept is not to speak of others' faults, and the thirteenth is not to praise oneself and disparage others. One year for Lent, I gave up saying bad things about other people. It was distressing how challenging this was. I often found myself slapping my hand over my mouth when a judgmental statement about someone was already halfway out.

The Sixteen Precepts

The Three Refuges
  1. I take refuge in Buddha.
  2. I take refuge in Dharma.
  3. I take refuge in Sangha.

The Three General Resolutions
  4. I resolve to avoid evil.
  5. I resolve to do good.
  6. I resolve to liberate all sentient beings.

The Ten Cardinal Precepts
  7. I resolve not to kill,
     but to cherish all life.
  8. I resolve not to take what is not given,
     but to respect the things of others.
  9. I resolve not to misuse sexuality,
     but to be caring and responsible.
10. I resolve not to lie,
     but to speak the truth.
11. I resolve not to cause others to abuse alcohol or drugs, nor to do so myself,
     but to keep the mind clear.
12. I resolve not to speak of the faults of others,
     but to be understanding and sympathetic.
13. I resolve not to praise myself and disparage others,
     but to overcome my own shortcomings.
14. I resolve not to withhold spiritual or material aid,
     but to give them freely when needed.
15. I resolve not to indulge in anger,
     but to practice forbearance.
16. I resolve not to revile the Three Treasures
     (Buddha, Dharma, and Sangha),
     but to cherish and uphold them.

Source: Rochester Zen Center, *Ethical Guidelines:* Part 1, "The Buddhist Precepts," available on-line at http://www.rzc.org/html/abc/ethical.pdf.

Like zazen, the precepts are a practice. We repeatedly notice when we are not following a precept and return to following the precept. We practice noticing not just our blatant departures from the precepts but also the small and subtle ways in which we wander away from fully living the precepts.

In *Getting Saved from the Sixties,* Steve Tipton, a sociologist of religion, argues that the main reason 1960s youth joined "alternative" religious movements like Zen was to try to make moral sense of their lives. They had been raised in a culture that combined a "biblical" ethic, characterized by obedience to authority and conforming to rules, with a "utilitarian individual" ethic, characterized by expediency and cost-benefit analysis, and they had reacted with the countercultural "expressive" ethic, characterized by intuitive response to situations. But none of these systems had quite worked for them, and in Zen, they found a satisfying synthesis of the cultural and countercultural ethics. Zen's ethic is "expressive" in understanding that an enlightened person will intuitively respond appropriately to situations, but it keeps this "expressiveness" from degenerating toward anarchy and egoism by prescribing a spiritual discipline to develop one's intuitive sensibilities and a set of rules to use as guidelines for one's behavior while one cannot yet count on intuition as a reliable guide.

C. S. Lewis suggests a similar way of understanding Christian morality. He says that the moral realm exists to be transcended. To be used as practical guidelines, he says, Christianity's two great commandments have to be understood as commanding us to act *as if* we loved God and neighbor. We can't *love* on command, but we can act *as if* we love. We can act in a loving way. But there's a problem here. On the one hand, if we only act *as if* we love, we are not obeying the command, and on the other hand, if we truly loved God and neighbor, there would be no issue of needing to obey a command. So, Lewis says, the command to love God and neighbor really tells us, "Ye must be born again." Until we are reborn, we act as if we loved—that is, we act morally. Lewis says, "There is no morality in Heaven. The angels never knew (from within) the meaning of the word *ought,* and the blessed dead have long since gladly forgotten it."

In Zen, we resolve to be bodhisattvas. From the absolute perspective, the bodhisattva sees that all beings are already buddhas and that our freedom is found right here in the midst of the big mess of life. This is wisdom. From the relative perspective, the bodhisattva sees all the pain and suffering in the world and is moved to do everything possible to clean up the mess and to help others realize their freedom within the mess. This is compassion. Rather than dwelling on the mountaintop of the absolute, the bodhisattva returns to the valley of the relative to liberate all beings.

Practicing with Everything

Any activity can be used for Zen practice. In counting the breath and following the breath, you notice thoughts and return to the breathing. In walking meditation, you notice thoughts and return to the walking. Anything can be practiced this way: repeatedly notice your wandering thoughts and return your attention to the activity at hand.

In the setting of a Zen monastery or retreat, everything *is* practiced this way, or at least one is encouraged to practice everything this way: sitting practice, walking practice, chanting practice, eating oatmeal practice, lawn mowing practice, carrot chopping practice, telephone answering practice, video editing practice, driving to the post office practice, jogging practice, even rest practice.

The more complicated the activity is and the more conceptual thought it requires, the more challenging it is to notice wandering thoughts and return one's attention to the activity. This is one reason that the tasks assigned during the work period at a Zen retreat tend to be simple, repetitive, physical tasks like weeding the garden, washing windows, peeling potatoes, or stuffing envelopes.

Toward the end of a Christian contemplative prayer retreat, the retreat leaders were saying a bit about the transition from silence to ordinary daily life. One of the participants, a Korean Baptist seminary professor, said slowly and in very broken English, "Here, I have been observing silence. Afterward, I will observe noise." Zen practitioners return regularly to the silence of zazen. Then the awareness being uncovered in zazen is gradually expanded to include all the activities of our noisy lives.

Anything Practice

To practice with any activity, just fill in the blank:

- Attend to _____.
- When you realize that your attention has wandered off, notice the thought and gently return your attention to _____.

Notice the thought,
return to _____,
notice the thought,
return to _____,
notice the thought,
return to _____, ...

Following are some examples of "anything practice." The list of resources at the back of the book includes a section on practicing with certain aspects of life that can be especially challenging: stress, pain, illness, depression, fear, anxiety, ambition, death, and dying.

Eating Practice

Pay attention to the food and to all the physical sensations involved in eating. What does the food look like? How does it smell? How does the utensil or the food feel in your hand? How do your hand and arm feel as you move your hand toward your mouth? How does the food feel in your mouth? What does it taste like? How does your tongue move as you chew? What does it sound like when you chew? What does it feel like when you swallow? When do you get the impulse to reach for another bite of food? What does that impulse feel like? How does your hand move?

When you realize you are no longer attending to your eating but are caught up in thoughts—and this includes thoughts about eating, like "This could've used more garlic," "Home-grown tomatoes are so much better than store-bought," "Why does he always overcook the eggs?"—notice the thought and gently return your attention to the physical sensations of eating.

- Attend to the physical sensations of eating.
- When you realize that your attention has wandered off, notice the thought and gently return your attention to the physical sensations of eating.

Notice the thought,
return to eating,
notice the thought,
return to eating,
notice the thought,
return to eating, . . .

Listening Practice

In some of the meditation groups I've led, we share observations and thoughts about our practice with other members of the group. During these conversations, we do "listening practice":

- Look at the person who is speaking, and listen to what he or she is saying.
- When you realize that your attention has wandered off, notice the thought and gently return your attention to listening.

Notice the thought,
return to listening,
notice the thought,
return to listening,
notice the thought,
return to listening, . . .

Try this with your family, friends, coworkers—anyone. (My husband would be grateful if I did this practice more often with him!)

Practicing with Pain

Practicing with pain is, I think, one of the first ways in which many Zen practitioners get a taste of what no-self really means. When we let go of a self-centered view of reality, there is no longer *me* suffering from *pain;* there is simply pain. The separation of "me" from "not me" is what gives rise to suffering—our own suffering and the suffering we cause others.

When pain arises—when, for instance, your knees begin to hurt as you do zazen—instead of squirming and fidgeting and trying to escape the pain, try sitting still with the pain, both physically and mentally. Open your compassionate awareness to the pain. Let the pain in instead of trying to keep it out. Sink into the pain as you would sink into a hot bath. Experience the pain fully. Where exactly do you feel it? Does it feel sharp, dull, throbbing, tight, achy, tingly, warm? Does the sensation remain constant, or does it change? Let the whole universe be the pain. Become only the experience of pain. *Be* the pain.

At least for a moment, you may get a taste of being in pain without suffering from the pain. It's not that the pain goes away or that the pain is no longer painful but that the pain is OK. The pain just is.

When you notice that you are separating yourself from the pain and are caught up in thoughts—and this includes thoughts about the pain, like "I hate pain," "I don't know how much longer I can take this," "I'll never be able to walk again," "'*Be* the pain'? What's *that* supposed to mean?"—notice the thought and gently return your attention to the physical sensations of the pain.

- Attend to the physical sensations of the pain. Open your compassionate awareness to the pain. *Be* the pain.
- When you realize that you are thinking about the pain—separating from the pain—or are caught up in some other thought, notice the thought and gently return your attention to the physical sensations of the pain.

Notice the thought,
   return to the physical sensations of the pain,
      notice the thought,
         return to the physical sensations of the pain,
            notice the thought,
               return to the physical sensations of
                  the pain, . . .

Practicing with pain does not mean being masochistic, fatalistic, passive, or stupid about pain. If you get appendicitis, you go straight to the hospital for an appendectomy *and* you practice with the pain while you're waiting for surgery and while you're healing. If you're suffering from depression, you get it treated *and* you practice with whatever depression is still present—opening compassionate awareness to it instead of separating from it. If you always have knee pain when you do zazen, you do what you can to alleviate the pain—you get some advice on your sitting posture, maybe learn some stretching exercises, maybe choose to sit in a chair instead of on the floor—*and* you practice with whatever knee pain you do experience. Practicing with pain in no way precludes trying to prevent or alleviate pain. It isn't necessarily easy to get the knack of simultaneously trying to change a situation and opening compassionate awareness to it exactly as it is. It can feel like there's a tension there or even a contradiction, but there doesn't have to be.

Pain can be a useful thing to practice with, but this doesn't mean that you should go out of your way to experience pain or that you shouldn't try to relieve pain. As my husband likes to point out, this life has no shortage of pain, so you needn't worry that you'll run short and have none left to practice with. Please do all you can to free yourself and others from pain. This is a vital part of the practice of compassion.

Daydreaming Practice?

My friend Jennifer asked me if there is such a thing as daydreaming practice. Can you daydream mindfully? I found this an entertaining question to ponder, and here's what I came up with.

I considered whether mindful daydreaming is exactly what Zen practice is. That is, we're usually busy daydreaming, but in Zen we repeatedly notice that we're daydreaming and return our attention to the present moment. But that's probably understanding daydreaming too broadly.

Daydreaming might be better understood as one among many species of things our minds do other than attending to the present moment—distinguishing daydreaming from, say, obsessing about a relationship, planning the meeting you're leading on Tuesday, or rehashing that horrible scene with your brother. I'm imagining daydreaming as the kind of thing you might do while sitting on a porch swing on a lazy summer afternoon—letting your mind drift idly and pleasantly.

So if you want to daydream mindfully, you let your mind drift idly and pleasantly, and when you notice that you've wandered from idle, pleasant thoughts to worrying thoughts or vengeful thoughts, mentally creating to-do lists, or anything else that's too unpleasant or project-oriented, notice those thoughts, let them go, and return to the idle, pleasant drifting.

Maybe that's what "daydreaming practice" is.

5

Making Zen Practice
Part of Your Life

Developing a Regular Zen Practice

If you want to have a regular Zen practice, I would encourage
you to make zazen a habit, a part of your daily routine,
like brushing your teeth. It would be a bother if every time you
brushed your teeth, you had to psych yourself up for it, remind
yourself of the value of toothbrushing for the health of your
teeth and gums, and decide what would be the best time for it
that day. It's just not that big a deal, and neither is zazen. And
your daily sitting need not take more time than making and
drinking your cup of coffee or taking your morning shower.
Just sit down at about the same time every day for five or ten
minutes and count your breath—every morning before you
have your cereal or every afternoon before the kids get home
from school or every evening at your desk just after you've shut
down your computer for the day or every night after you're in
your pajamas or whatever works for you.

If you have a regular prayer time each day, you can add your meditation time onto that. You might find that doing zazen before you pray can be a way to let go of the mental chatter a bit so that you can be more attentive in your prayer time. Or you might find that you prefer to start with verbal prayer and then, when you've turned the particular issues of the day over to God, you can settle down to simply being there.

To encourage your meditation habit, you might want to set aside a corner of a room especially for this: a small space that is clean and attractive, with your meditation cushion or bench or chair, perhaps a candle, some incense, some flowers.

When I sit alone, I decide ahead of time how long I'm going to sit and always sit for that full length of time, or longer if I'm so inclined, but I don't quit before the end of the time I've decided on. Having made this commitment to myself spares me from spending any of my sitting time deciding when to stop or considering whether to cut the period short. I just sit for however long I've decided to sit, and that's that. And knowing that I'm committed to sitting for the full period I've decided on encourages me to choose reasonable lengths of time instead of getting overly ambitious about it and then feeling disappointed with myself for quitting early.

Now that I've given you all that good advice, let me admit that while other people, including my husband, are self-disciplined enough to maintain a regular Zen practice on their own, generally I'm not, and I know I'm not at all unusual in this. I suspect that those of us who need some external help to maintain a spiritual practice are in the majority.

There was a stretch of about half a year once, between my three-month residency at the Zen monastery and my year's residency, when I sat at home alone four or five times a week for about twenty minutes at a time, but that's one of the few times I've managed to have a regular meditation practice without some sort of external structure or accountability.

I first had a regular meditation practice when I was taking a meditation class at the Naropa Institute in Boulder. The class was structured like a regular college class. Twice a week we had lectures, which were actually dharma talks. Once a week we met in small discussion sections to talk about our practice. For homework we had some reading assignments, and we were expected to do something like seven hours of sitting a week. I knew I'd never manage that, so to forestall my inevitable guilt, I adjusted my own requirement down to four hours a week. We had to keep a record of how long we sat each day in a little calendar, like a flight log or a calorie counter, and we met once a week individually with a meditation instructor. I had a regular meditation practice while I was taking that class.

At Zen Mountain Monastery, we did two thirty-five-minute periods of zazen at dawn and two at night, except during the winter quarter, when dawn zazen was optional and I opted to sleep in, and during the monthly weeklong sesshin, when we sat about eight hours a day. If you weren't in the *zendo*—the meditation hall—when you were supposed to be, one of the monastics would come find you. I had a regular meditation practice then, although that was a lot more sitting than I really wanted to do, and I felt like I was in the zendo under duress a lot of the time.

In 1999, Brian and I moved to an apartment two blocks from the Atlanta Soto Zen Center. Brian was in charge of opening the place up and timing the sitting periods on Monday mornings, and he was often there for zazen several other times a week. I sat at the Zen center maybe four or five times in the two and a half years we lived there.

One year for Lent, in addition to giving up sweets, I decided I'd sit for at least five minutes a day. That seemed like a reasonable, minimal sort of spiritual discipline to take on. I stuck with the abstention from sweets for the whole forty days—difficult as that is for me—but the sitting fell by the wayside within a week.

I had a regular Zen practice when I was simultaneously helping run the Zen group at Emory University and leading two Zen for Christians groups at churches. I had to show up in the basement of the Emory chapel every Monday afternoon, in the parlor of Glenn Memorial United Methodist Church every Monday night, and in the middle school room of Central Congregational UCC every Tuesday night. So I sat three times a week, for two periods of about twenty minutes each. This is one of the things I like about teaching Zen to other people: I sit myself. I don't have *decide* to sit; I just show up where I'm supposed to be, and once I'm sitting there on a zafu and have rung the bell to start a sitting period, I might as well do zazen along with everyone else.

As I write this, I have a regular practice. Brian and I are living at a Christian retreat center, and the daily prayer services include periods of silence, which I usually use for zazen, and occasionally I go to the chapel a little early or stay a little late for some additional silent time. I've had no problem keeping up this discipline of meditation. I just show up in the chapel when I'm supposed to, and when there's silence, I do zazen. We also eat many of our meals in silence, which is conducive to eating mindfully.

The moral of my story is, if you want to have a regular meditation practice, you may find it helpful to make a commitment to sitting regularly with a group. And even if you do sit regularly on your own, it can be valuable to sit with a group also.

It helps to have the support of others sitting with you. Sitting alone, it's much easier to let yourself fidget or quit early or get up to answer the phone or decide that this would be a good time to pay the bills or clean out the garage or alphabetize the spice rack. Also, there's a sort of synergy I can't quite explain that happens when you're sitting with a group of people who are all practicing quietness, stillness, and attentiveness. And of course it's nice to get to know some other people who share your commitment, who will be supportive of your practice, with whom you can talk about practice.

For many years, Brian was part of a group in Boulder that met every Monday evening at a Mennonite church to sit silently for half an hour, to discuss issues of peace and social justice, and to support each other's commitments and actions. The members of the "Monday group" were of different religions or no religion, and they weren't all doing the same practice of silent meditation or prayer, but they all wanted time to sit in silence with like-minded people.

There are suggestions in the list of resources at the end of the book for finding a meditation group, or you can start your own.

Practicing at a Zen Center

One of the main things that happens at Zen centers is zazen. Zen centers generally offer meditation sessions at least a few times a week, typically consisting of two or more sitting periods of twenty-five to forty minutes each, separated by brief periods of walking meditation. The meditation is usually preceded or followed by a bit of chanting. And Zen centers often have an extended Sunday-morning program, including zazen, chanting, a talk, and an opportunity to meet one-on-one with a teacher.

Chanting

Zen chanting is done on a single low note—actually two notes an octave apart, for the higher and lower voices—in a steady rhythm, speeding up gradually as it goes along. The beat is kept with a large wooden drum called a *mokugyo* that looks like a giant fish (though I might never have realized it was a fish if I hadn't been told). The mokugyo makes a low, resonant thoomp, thoomp, thoomp.

Chanting is not about the meaning of the words being chanted but about the activity of chanting. Chanting is a practice like any other Zen practice. You notice your wandering thoughts and return your attention to the physical sensations of the chanting—to the sounds and vibrations of your own voice, the other voices, and the drum. You chant from the hara, from the belly, and blend your voice with the other voices so that they are not separate.

The Heart Sutra, which is one of the most famous and most widely used Buddhist texts, is chanted regularly at Zen centers. A *sutra* is understood to record the teachings of the Buddha. The Heart Sutra is about a page long and is considered the heart, or essence, of the voluminous "Perfection of Wisdom" literature of Buddhism. The Heart Sutra focuses on *shunyata,* or emptiness, which is an extension of the teaching of no-self. Not only human beings but all beings and all things are empty of "self," empty of any inherent, independent, separate existence. Things do really exist but not in the way we tend to think they do. The heart of the Heart Sutra is the line "Form is emptiness; emptiness is form." Form, or physical reality, is empty of inherent existence, and emptiness cannot be discovered apart from form. Form and emptiness are two appearances of the same reality. From the relative perspective, we see form; from the absolute perspective, we see emptiness. Even the teachings of Buddhism, which are useful from the relative perspective, are ultimately empty, and the Heart Sutra negates one Buddhist teaching after another. For example, it says that "in emptiness" there is "no suffering, no cause of suffering, no extinguishing, no path." That is, even the Four Noble Truths are ultimately empty. Realizing the emptiness of all things, the bodhisattva lives "far beyond deluded thoughts" and without fear—in nirvana.

The Four Bodhisattva Vows are also chanted regularly at Zen centers:

However innumerable all beings are,
  I vow to save them all.
However inexhaustible my delusions are,
  I vow to extinguish them all.
However immeasurable the Dharma teachings are,
  I vow to master them all.
However endless the Buddha's Way is,
  I vow to follow it completely.

In resolving to attain these apparently unattainable goals, we reaffirm a commitment to Zen practice. But again, while chanting the Four Vows or the Heart Sutra or any other text, you don't ponder the meaning of what you're chanting; you just chant.

Bowing

There is a lot of bowing at Zen centers—to the Buddha, to the teacher, to the sangha, and even to the place where you sit.

A bow is done with the palms together, fingers pointing up, and fingertips a few inches in front of the nose—a gesture called *gassho.* With the hands in gassho, you bow from the waist, keeping the back straight. Some Zen centers use only seated and standing bows. Other Zen centers also use full bows. A full bow begins with a standing bow; then you put both knees on the floor, touch your forehead to the floor, touch the backs of your hands to the floor on either side of your head, and raise your palms an inch or two—as if lifting the feet of the Buddha, I've been told.

Bowing is not worship but rather a practice of gratitude and nonduality. In Zen, we bow to the Buddha in gratitude for his teachings and to express that we and the Buddha are not separate, that each of us is a buddha. We bow to the teacher and to the sangha in gratitude for a guide on the way and companions on the way, and we bow to express our nonduality with the teacher and the sangha. We bow to our zafu in gratitude for a place to sit and the opportunity to sit. Among Zen practitioners, bows are often used in place of "thank you" and "you're welcome."

The Kyosaku

An aspect of Zen training that may at first seem strange or offputting is the use of the *kyosaku,* the "awakening stick" or "encouragement stick."

During sitting periods, a monitor may make the rounds of the zendo, walking slowly and quietly behind the rows of sitters and stopping to adjust people's posture if necessary—for example, straightening a back that's leaning to one side or pulling back shoulders that are slumped forward. The monitor carries a kyosaku—a long, thin, flat wooden stick. If you request the kyosaku by putting your hands together in gassho, the monitor will give you a good hard whack on each shoulder with the kyosaku, on an acupressure point between the shoulder blade and neck. This hurts, but it can release tension in the shoulders and back, and it can help revive you if you're drowsy. It can also be a spur to greater alertness or deeper practice. And the kyosaku makes a loud, sharp noise that lends a crisp, alert atmosphere to the zendo.

Like everything in Zen, the kyosaku is meant to be an aid to practice, but if you know that being hit with a stick would not help but hinder your practice, you simply need not request it.

Dokusan

Zen centers usually have designated times during the week when you can meet with a teacher one on one to talk about your practice. These meetings—variously called *dokusan, daisan,* or "interview"—happen during sitting periods.

Each center has its own particular procedure for dokusan, but it typically goes something like this. The teacher, who is in another room, rings a bell to indicate that the student may enter. After a bow or series of bows, the student kneels on a zabuton, facing the teacher, almost knee to knee, and says, "My name is _____, and my practice is _____." For example, "My name is Kim, and my practice is counting the breath." After that, the interaction is completely free-form. The student can ask a question about practice or present his or her insight to the teacher, who will respond. The teacher doesn't generally initiate anything. If the student doesn't have anything to say, the teacher probably won't have anything to say either. The teacher is there to answer questions, to bring you back on course if you're going way off, and to act as a mirror for your practice—that is, to help you see where you are. These meetings tend to be brief, ranging from a few seconds to five minutes. (I've occasionally taken as much as half an hour.) The teacher ends the interview by ringing the bell, which is the signal for one student to leave and the next to come in.

Dharma Talks

Regularly at Zen centers, usually weekly, a talk is given by the teacher or another member of the sangha. Sometimes these talks explain an aspect of the practice or teachings of Zen, but the traditional dharma talk, or *teisho,* is a different sort of presentation. The teisho is usually based on a koan, but it is not mainly an explanation of the koan or a commentary on the koan. In a teisho, the teacher is not trying to convey information but to give expression to the direct experience of the ultimate nature of reality and to speak directly to the students' inherently awakened nature. The language of the teisho is often paradoxical or poetic, like the language of koans. As Zen teacher John Daido Loori says, dharma talks are "dark to the mind but radiant to the heart."

Caricatures of Christianity

If you visit a Zen center or read more about Zen, you may encounter some caricatures of Christianity and prejudices about

Christianity, either subtle or explicit. More than half of the Zen practitioners in the United States are from Christian backgrounds, and while some of them are practicing Christians, most are not. Since the former Christians were often attracted to Zen in part because of its differences from the Christianity they knew, they can find it puzzling to encounter Zen practitioners who are Christian.

You may hear, from Zen teachers or other Zen practitioners, that Zen is more intellectually satisfying than Christianity, that Christianity is too judgmental and moralistic, that Christianity focuses on belief to the neglect of religious experience, that Christianity confuses mythical and factual language, that Christianity is too hierarchical, or that Christianity is dualistic. (I'm not entirely sure what is meant by "dualistic," but I think the idea is that Christianity understands God as a being who is entirely separate and distinct from human beings and the rest of creation.) Of course, these statements are unfair. They are mistaken generalizations from particular manifestations of Christianity, or they reveal an uninformed or unsophisticated understanding of Christianity. Such statements can be taken as an opportunity to offer a bit of religious education and, in some cases, a bit of pastoral care to a wounded former Christian.

The Catholic church my husband belonged to in Boulder sponsored an event that was officially called something like Apology Night but unofficially called We're Sorry We Screwed You Up Night. Former and "lapsed" Catholics were invited to come tell church representatives how they'd been hurt by the church and were promised that these representatives would simply listen and apologize—no arguments, no excuses, no attempts at reevangelization. As a Christian at a Zen center, you might on occasion feel like you're the representative of Christianity at We're Sorry We Screwed You Up Night. And perhaps the most helpful thing you can do is simply to listen and, if it seems appropriate, offer an apology.

Community

If you're going to a Zen center looking for the sense of community that you can find at many churches, you may find it, but you may not. Since Zen practitioners mainly sit in silence together and do a little chanting together, you may sit with people for months before you have occasion even to learn their names.

Brian and I had been participating in the Thursday-evening sitting of a small Zen group in Boulder for maybe half a year when we were invited to a picnic. It had been about two years since the group had planned a social event, and they had decided it was about time for another one. And one of the members of the group invited us to a party at his house once. Those are the only two times we socialized with other members of that Zen group.

But even without much ordinary social interaction, you may develop a special sense of connection with the people you sit with regularly, especially if you do sesshin together.

Sesshin

The sesshin, or silent, intensive meditation retreat, is the heart of Zen training. Even Western Zen centers that have stripped Zen down to its bare bones offer sesshins, lasting from a day to a week. The primary activity of sesshin is zazen—about eight hours a day, usually in blocks of two or three sitting periods of about thirty minutes each. The blocks of sitting are interspersed with meals, chanting, dharma talks, a short work period, and some time to rest. Usually, some of the meals during sesshin are eaten in the zendo in an elaborate ritual called *oryoki* (pronounced like "Oreo cookie" without the "coo-") that encourages the continued practice of attention to the present moment and also an appreciation for our food and the labors that go into bringing us our food. During sesshin, there are daily dharma talks and daily opportunities to meet with a teacher in dokusan.

The Japanese word *sesshin* literally means "collecting the heart-mind." (*Shin* can be translated as "heart," "mind," "spirit," or "consciousness," among other things.) Sesshin is an intensive and extended opportunity to collect one's scattered attention and practice awareness of the present moment. In one sense, you are all alone with yourself during sesshin, collecting your own heart-mind, but you are also part of a group of people who are practicing collectively—sitting together, walking together, chanting together, eating together, working together.

Sesshin is a challenging practice, both physically and mentally. It's not easy to sit still with one's body and mind for an extended period. But there seems to be a consensus among

Zen practitioners that the first two days of a sesshin are generally the most difficult, and then you settle in and get into the swing of it. (This is a problem with one-day and weekend sesshins: you only get the hardest part.) When I was living at the Zen monastery, I was always relieved when sesshin was over, but by the time the next sesshin came around three weeks later, I was ready to intensify my practice again.

At the end of sesshin, the participants tend to look all bright and shiny. This may be in part because everyone is high on endorphins from sitting still with physical pain, but I don't think that's all it is. After many days of noticing wandering thoughts and returning to the present moment, one's attachments and aversions lose some of their force, and one is more prone simply to attend to and appreciate each moment.

Sesshin is an especially good opportunity to practice and experience the liberation from "self" and suffering that the Buddha taught—to practice and experience our inherent freedom to live a life of joy and compassion.

Practice

Zazen: *Shikantaza*, or "Just Sitting"

The Japanese word *shikantaza* means "nothing but precisely sitting" or, more succinctly, "just sitting." Shikantaza is, in a way, the "purest" form of zazen. There is no technique, nothing to do. We do not sit in order to become enlightened or in order to become anything. We just sit. We sit as a manifestation of our inherent enlightenment, and we sit in the faith that we will one day realize our inherent enlightenment.

We are unaccustomed to doing nothing. In counting the breath, we are doing a little something that helps us approximate doing nothing. Following the breath is a closer approximation of doing nothing. And shikantaza *is* doing nothing.

Shikantaza is both the easiest Zen practice to explain and also the most difficult to explain. Here are the directions:

• Just sit.

Or if you'd like a little more elaboration:

• Take the posture, and just sit and be aware.

That's it. But since I know that these directions, though simple, can be mystifying, I'll say a bit more.

In all the other forms of Zen practice described in this book, you focus your attention on something in particular—breathing, walking, eating, or whatever—and when you realize that your attention has wandered off, you notice the thought and return your attention to that something in particular. Shikantaza is different in two ways. First, the attention is not focused but opened to include everything happening right here and now in the space where you're sitting. Second, thoughts are not treated differently from physical sensations. You don't "return from" the thoughts "to" the physical sensations. It's all just something to notice. Both the thoughts and the physical sensations, both the "inner" and the "outer," are part of what's happening here and now. In Buddhist psychology, there are six senses: the five that Westerners traditionally count—sight, hearing, smell, taste, and touch—plus mind. Just as the object of hearing is sound, the object of mind is thought. In shikantaza, you observe the entire flow of consciousness, the objects of all six senses.

In shikantaza, you just sit, aware, observing whatever floats through consciousness. Let it all be. Let it come in, and let it go out. Don't grab on to thoughts and sensations, and don't push them away. Just observe them. Most of the time, we grab on to our thoughts and sensations or we push them away. We get involved in attachment or aversion. In shikantaza, we just sit here and observe. And when we do cling to thoughts or push them away, we just sit here and observe that.

So the practice of shikantaza might go something like this:

I notice the feel of the air expanding my belly. I notice the sound of a bus going by outside the Zen center. I notice the fidgeting of the person on my left. I notice my annoyance at the fidgeting of the person on my left. I notice the feel of my lungs expanding and contracting as I breathe. I notice my eyes itching because of my allergies. I notice that I just spent several minutes rehearsing a phone conversation with my mother. I notice the feel of my breathing in my hara. I notice the feel of the waistband of my pants against my belly. I notice the tension in my shoulders. I notice my restlessness. I notice the feel of the breath coming in and out of my nose. I notice the feel of my breathing in my hara. I notice the thought that maybe I should leave the Zen center right after the talk, instead of staying for two more sitting periods. I notice my wish that my mind were quieter today. I notice the feel of my thumbs touching together. I notice the feel of my breathing in my hara. I notice that I'm controlling my breathing. I notice my thoughts about what a hard time I have letting go of my breathing. I notice my eyes itching because of my allergies. I notice the smell of the incense. I notice the sound of a motorcycle going by. I notice my thoughts about whether I need to get the oil changed soon and whether I need to stop by the market this afternoon. I notice my feeling that these chores are burdensome. I notice that I was just putting my experience of zazen into words because I want to describe it in my writing. I notice the feel of my breathing in my hara. . . .

Shikantaza is a difficult practice. Even though there's nothing to do, it requires a certain state of mind. Yasutani Roshi says, "You must sit with a mind which is alert and at the same time unhurried and composed. This mind must be like a well-tuned piano string: taut but not overtight." If counting the breath is like riding a bicycle with training wheels, and following the breath is like riding a bicycle without training wheels, then shikantaza is like riding a unicycle. There's no support at all. I'd recommend beginning with the bicycle, but when you get the hang of that, you might want to try the unicycle.

The Essentials of *Shikantaza*

- Find a sitting posture that allows you to have an upright spine and to be stable and completely still.

- Keep your eyes open, with your gaze lowered at about a 45-degree angle, soft-focused, eyelids droopy.

- Take one or two slow, deep breaths. Then let your breath be however it is.

- Let your attention settle in your *hara* (about two inches below the navel).

- Optional: Spend a few minutes counting the breath, to settle in.

- Let your awareness expand to include the entire flow of consciousness.

> *Notice whatever is happening right now,*
>> *and now,*
>>> *and now,*
>>>> *and now,*
>>>>> *and now,*
>>>>>> *and now . . .*

The Changing Weather

Here is an image that has helped me feel how to just sit and be aware of whatever is here.

Sometimes I see myself as a mountain, massive and solid and stable, rooted in the earth, surrounded by wide open sky. And my thoughts are clouds moving by the mountaintop. Sometimes they're just wispy little clouds, and the bright, clear sunlight shining down on the mountaintop is hardly blocked at all by the passing clouds. I feel the sun shining warmly on me in the thin, dry air. I feel the spaciousness of the sky. Sometimes huge storm systems blow through so that the mountaintop is completely obscured by storm clouds and rain. But the storms always pass. And they always return. Clouds, clear sky, clouds, clear sky, rain and thunder and lightning and hail, clear sky, clouds, clear sky—I feel the rhythm of the changing weather. The sun is always shining, whether the sunlight reaches the mountaintop or not. The sky is always clear above the clouds. All the weather, "good" and "bad," happens within the wide open space. And the mountain is just here.

Our job when we sit is to be the mountain, to experience all the changing weather in the wide open space, whether it's gray and cold, sunny and warm, noisy and scary, or cool and invigorating. Just experience it all. Be it all. Be a mountain in the bright, warm sun. Be a mountain in the cold, wet rain. Perhaps you prefer the sunny times to the rainy times. That's fine. Just experience that. Be that.

I'd like to warn you about two common misunderstandings here. These apply not just to the practice of shikantaza but to all forms of Zen practice.

First, please note that Zen practice is not about climate control. It's not about making all your weather seventy-five degrees and sunny. I think you know that that's impossible anyway. I suspect that you would not be exploring Zen unless you had begun to face that scary fact about life: that no matter what you do—no matter *what*—there will always be storms. The good news is, that's absolutely fine. The sun and the storms—it's all OK. Our preference for sun rather than storms—that's OK too. The end of suffering that the Buddha taught is not liberation *from* the storms but liberation *in* the storms—and in the sun. It is not necessary to control the weather.

A second common misunderstanding is that Zen practice is about indifference to storms. But that's not it either. Zen practice is not about indifference to the weather. It's not about not caring about the weather, having no preference about the weather, insulating ourselves from the weather or from our feelings about the weather. That's not liberation or equanimity; that's depression. Or else it's what Yasutani Roshi calls "it-doesn't-matter Zen with no practice and no enlightenment." We are not liberated *from* our dislike of sweltering heat or our enjoyment of powdery new snow; we are liberated *within* this human life, including our feelings and preferences.

One winter night in Boulder, my friend Anne and I were walking home from the grocery store on snow-packed streets, with the temperature in the teens. Anne is from San Diego and I'm from Los Angeles, and we both hated this weather and were really unhappy about being so cold. Then we thought, What would the Zen attitude be? Our first thought was that we were supposed to be OK with this weather, but then we realized that that wasn't it. Rather, it was that we could be OK with how much we hated this weather. So we happily hated the weather the rest of the way home—yucky, icky, nasty cold weather!

Zen practice is not about controlling the weather; nor is it about indifference to the weather. It's about awareness of the weather. Experience the endlessly changing weather. *Be* the endlessly changing weather.

The Flowing Stream

Here's another image.

Sometimes I imagine my mind as a stream. When my mind is busy and noisy, those are the rough, tumbling, noisy places in the stream, the places where the water is flowing over a jumble of rocks, where it's all white and foamy. And when my mind is relatively still and open and quiet, those are the clear, calm places in the stream, the places where the stream bed is smooth and flat, where you can see right through the water to the bottom. I just flow along—rough and noisy, then clear and quiet, then rough and noisy and rough and noisy and rough and noisy, then clear and quiet.

All of it is fine. The rough parts are not "bad." They do not need to be eliminated. Zen practice is not about steamrolling the bottom of the stream nice and flat to eliminate the white water. It's about the freedom of simply being the flowing stream, with all its variations. Of course, sometimes we dearly, desperately wish that we could steamroll the bottom of the stream. Sometimes the rough parts of the stream do not *feel* like they're fine at all. That's fine too. Those feelings do not need to be eliminated either. They are another natural variation in the flowing stream.

We just flow along, opening compassionate awareness to all the variations in the stream.

One More Thought

If It's Worth Doing, It's Worth Doing Badly

You've probably heard the aphorism, "If it's worth doing, it's worth doing right." I suppose there are people who need to hear that, but I'm not one of them, and I suspect you're not one of them either. Zen seems to attract a lot of perfectionistic, self-critical types who think we should do everything "right." This attitude tends to have the unfortunate side effect that there are many worthwhile things we don't do at all rather than doing them "wrong." If you approach Zen practice with this attitude, you may not practice at all, or you may practice only in occasional, exhausting bursts of "excellence."

So I would like to commend to you an alternative aphorism: *If it's worth doing, it's worth doing badly.*

I discovered this bit of practical wisdom about ten years ago, in a magazine article called "The Joys of Mediocrity: Anything Worth Doing Is Worth Doing Badly." The author had recently realized that her perfectionism had been squelching her enjoyment of life. So following the example of her husband, who had great fun playing the tuba badly, she had let go of her need to do everything well and was having great fun dancing badly.

Some years later, I learned that it was G. K. Chesterton who coined the saying "If a thing is worth doing, it is worth doing badly." In a book I was reading on prayer, the author quotes Chesterton and comments that prayer, which is worth doing, "requires the humility to attempt it knowing we will be clumsy."

I was reminded of this again when I heard a tape of a sermon by Fred Craddock, a well-known preacher whom my husband and I really like. The writer of the Letter to the Hebrews, Craddock says, is trying desperately, though not always gracefully or heartwarmingly, to save the church he is writing to, because he cares about that church. Craddock says, "It's been my observation that care frequently is raw, interferes, intrudes, says the wrong thing, has the wrong timing, disrupts, makes mistakes, frequently feels it needs to apologize. But one thing care never does. Care never lets anyone go completely." Caring is worth doing clumsily, inexpertly, imperfectly, rather than not at all.

If practicing meditation is worth doing, it's worth doing badly. If practicing compassion is worth doing, it's worth doing badly. You need not choose between practicing Zen "well" and not practicing Zen at all. Be a mediocre Zen practitioner, or a lousy Zen practitioner. Practice Zen awkwardly, sporadically, idiosyncratically. Do zazen in a noisy place with bright lights. Keep your eyes closed. Fidget. Slouch.

What we are practicing in Zen is the awareness that we have never been apart from our enlightened nature, that we cannot be apart from our enlightened nature. We are already buddhas. Sometimes we're fidgety buddhas, and sometimes we're still buddhas. Sometimes we're quiet buddhas, and sometimes we're chattery buddhas. Sometimes we're happy buddhas, and sometimes we're sad buddhas. Sometimes we're buddhas who think we should do everything perfectly, and sometimes we're buddhas who are willing to do things badly.

We open our compassionate awareness to all of it—now, and now, and now.

Recommended
Resources

Books

Zen Practice

The Three Pillars of Zen by Philip Kapleau   A helpful "how to"
    book, especially the introductory lectures on Zen training by
    Yasutani Roshi.

Everyday Zen by Charlotte Joko Beck   A straightforward and
    down-to-earth book about Zen practice in relation to every-
    day life, by the teacher at the Zen Center of San Diego.

Zen Mind, Beginner's Mind by Shunryu Suzuki   A beloved classic
    of American Zen, by the founder of the San Francisco Zen
    Center and the first Zen monastery in the United States,
    Tassajara, in Northern California.

Basic Buddhism

What the Buddha Taught by Walpola Rahula   A clear and concise introduction to basic Buddhist teachings (the Four Noble Truths, no-self, meditation, and so on) by a Buddhist monk and scholar.

Awakening the Buddha Within by Lama Surya Das   An introduction to Buddhism, organized around the Eightfold Path, by an American teacher of Tibetan Buddhism.

Radiant Mind: Essential Buddhist Teachings and Texts edited by Jean Smith   A well-chosen collection of classic Buddhist texts and commentaries by contemporary teachers in the meditation-oriented forms of Buddhism.

The Shambhala Dictionary of Buddhism and Zen   A useful reference book. Makes good browsing for learning more about Buddhism.

Practicing with _____

Full Catastrophe Living by Jon Kabat-Zinn   On practicing with stress, pain, and illness, by the founder and director of the Stress Reduction Clinic at the University of Massachusetts Medical Center.

The Depression Book and *The Fear Book* by Cheri Huber   On practicing with depression and fear or anxiety, by a Zen teacher.

Anger: Wisdom for Cooling the Flames by Thich Nhat Hanh   On practicing with anger, by a Zen teacher.

A Year to Live and other books by Stephen Levine   On practicing with death and dying, your own and others'.

Forgetting Ourselves on Purpose: Vocation and the Ethics of Ambition by Brian J. Mahan   On practicing with your ambitions and transmuting ambition into vocation. Written from a Christian and Zen perspective. (OK, so the author is my husband, but it really is a good book!)

Zen and Christianity

Zen Catholicism: A Suggestion by Dom Aelred Graham   A dense but well written and experientially oriented exploration of how Zen might help Catholics "realize more fully their own spiritual inheritance."

The Raft Is Not the Shore: Conversations Toward a Buddhist-Christian Awareness by Thich Nhat Hanh and Daniel Berrigan   Based on conversations in the 1970s between the two authors, a Zen teacher and a Jesuit priest, both involved in peace and justice work. Recently back in print.

Zen and the Birds of Appetite by Thomas Merton   A collection of essays on Zen and Christianity by a Trappist monk who was one of the great spiritual writers of the twentieth century. This book is more academic than a lot of Merton's writing.

Zen Gifts to Christians by Robert E. Kennedy   What Christians might learn from Zen. Kennedy is a Jesuit priest, a Zen teacher, a psychotherapist, and a professor of theology and Japanese.

Christian Contemplative Practice

The Cloud of Unknowing   A classic of Christian mysticism. A practical guide to contemplative prayer by an anonymous medieval author. Several translations are available; I like William Johnston's.

New Seeds of Contemplation by Thomas Merton   Wonderfully written reflections on the contemplative life, by a twentieth-century Trappist monk.

Open Mind, Open Heart: The Contemplative Dimension of the Gospel by Thomas Keating   Includes a brief history of Christian contemplative prayer and detailed instructions in "centering prayer."

The Way of a Pilgrim   The story of an anonymous nineteenth-century Russian peasant who wanted to "pray without ceasing" (I Thessalonians 5:17) and was introduced to the Jesus Prayer—the continuous repetition of "Lord Jesus Christ, Son of God, have mercy on me, a sinner"—a practice from the Orthodox Church, with roots in the desert spirituality of early Christianity. Several translations are available.

Web Sites

www.mro.com   The Web site of Zen Mountain Monastery includes beginning instruction in Zen meditation and "Cybermonk": e-mail your questions about Zen and get a reply from one of the monastics.

www.tricycle.com   The Web site of the Buddhist magazine *Tricycle* includes "Buddhist Basics" and a directory of Buddhist centers.

www.shalem.org   The Web site of the Shalem Institute for Spiritual Formation includes links to classic texts on contemplative practice from Christianity and other religious traditions.

www.centeringprayer.com   The Web site of Contemplative Outreach includes detailed instructions in centering prayer, writings on Christian contemplative prayer by Thomas Keating and others, and a list of contacts for centering prayer groups.

Sources of Meditation Cushions and Benches, Buddhist Books and Tapes, Bells, Incense, and Other Supplies

Carolina Morning Designs   Cushions, benches, and bells only. Request a brochure: (888) 267-5366 or cmd@zafu.net. On-line catalogue: www.zafu.net. Also on the Web site: "What's Wrong with the Chair?"

Dharma Communications   Request a catalogue: (845) 688-7993; dharmacom@dharma.net; or P.O. Box 156, Mt. Tremper, NY 12457. On-line catalogue: www.mro.org/dc/store.shtml.

DharmaCrafts   Request a catalogue: (800) 794-9862; customer_service @dharmacrafts.com; or 405 Waltham Street, Suite 234, Lexington, MA 02421. On-line catalogue: www.dharmacrafts.com.

Shasta Abbey Buddhist Supplies   Request a catalogue: (800) 653-3315; supplies@buddhistsupplies.com; or P.O. Box 1163, Mt. Shasta, CA 96067. On-line catalogue: www.buddhistsupplies.com. Offerings include a foam wedge to support sitting in a chair.

Finding a Meditation Group

Suggestions for finding a Zen center in your area:

1. Look in the Yellow Pages under "Meditation" or "Churches: Buddhist" or in the white pages under "Zen" (many Zen centers are called "Zen Center of [*location*]").

2. Browse the on-line directories of worldwide Buddhist centers at www.tricycle.com, www.buddhanet.net, and www.manjushri.com.

3. Browse *The Complete Guide to Buddhist America* by Don Morreale or *The Buddhist Directory* by Peter Lorie and Julie Foakes, which are directories of Buddhist centers in the United States and Canada, or *Journey of Awakening* by Ram Dass, which includes a directory of meditation centers.

You can use the same strategies to find a Tibetan, Vipassana, or Theravada Buddhist center. The practice taught to beginners in these traditions is quite similar to Zen meditation. There are more than a hundred Shambhala Meditation Centers in North America (and others around the world), offering meditation instruction in the Tibetan Buddhist tradition and through Shambhala Training, a secular path of meditation training. Contact Shambhala at (902) 420-1118 (in Nova Scotia) or info@shambhala.org, or see the lists of "Shambhala Centers" and "Practice Centers" on the Web site: www.shambhala.org.

Jesuit priest and Zen teacher Robert Kennedy leads Zen retreats around the country. For information, contact R. O'Connell at roconnell8@aol.com or (212) 831-5710, or go to Kennedy's Web site: kennedyzen.tripod.com.

To find a centering prayer group in your area, contact Contemplative Outreach at (973) 838-3384 (in New Jersey) or office@coutreach.org, or see the list of "Contacts" on the Web site: www.centeringprayer.com.

Notes

An Invitation to Zen Practice

1   *just plain Zen*   More precisely, the Zen in this book is just plain American Zen.

2   *like comparing tennis and mathematics*   Thomas Merton, *Zen and the Birds of Appetite* (New York: New Directions, 1968), p. 33.

3   *differential equations*   Thanks to my mathematician friend Fred Helenius for this suggestion of what mathematicians might ponder.

3   *"Thy will be done"—not my will, but thine*   The idea of connecting "Thy will be done" with Zen is from the chapter "Thy Will Be Done" in Charlotte Joko Beck, *Everyday Zen* (San Francisco: HarperSanFrancisco, 1989), pp. 201–203.

Practice: Zazen: Counting the Breath

13   *"a simplified space"*   Beck, *Everyday Zen,* p. 25.

19   *"In returning and rest . . ."*   Isaiah 30:15b–16.

Chapter One: How I Became a Christian Zen Practitioner

29   *"I felt as if . . ." and "Why people think . . ."*   I am quoting from a photocopy given to my husband, with a handwritten note citing Susan Howatch, *Church Times* (London), Jan. 1991.

36 *the aliens needed to* leave *the Vatican* Thanks to Helen Blier for this remark.

40 *"If you think your heart cannot pray, . . ."* Karl Rahner, *The Need and the Blessing of Prayer,* trans. Bruce W. Gillette (Collegeville, Minn.: Liturgical Press, 1997), p. 11. Other books on prayer that I have found especially helpful are C. S. Lewis, *Letters to Malcolm: Chiefly on Prayer* (Orlando, Fla.: Harcourt, 1973); Ann Ulanov and Barry Ulanov, *Primary Speech: A Psychology of Prayer* (Louisville, Ky.: Westminster/John Knox, 1982); and Anthony Bloom, *Beginning to Pray* (Mahwah, N.J.: Paulist Press, 1970).

40 *opening our hearts to God* Rahner, *The Need and the Blessing of Prayer,* p. 3.

41 *We heed God's call in Psalm 46* This way of describing contemplative prayer is from Tilden Edwards, *Living in the Presence: Disciplines for the Spiritual Heart* (San Francisco: HarperSanFrancisco, 1987), p. 11.

Practice: Walking Meditation

46 *"you feel as if . . ."* Shunryu Suzuki, *Zen Mind, Beginner's Mind* (New York: Weatherhill, 1973), p. 27.

Chapter Two: The Buddhist Way of Liberation from Suffering

49 *Siddhartha Gautama* For the story of the Buddha, I have drawn on Roger J. Corless, *The Vision of Buddhism* (New York: Paragon House, 1989), pp. 3–15; Peter Harvey, *An Introduction to Buddhism: Teachings, History and Practices* (Cambridge: Cambridge University Press, 1990), pp. 14–29; Damien Keown, *Buddhism: A Very Short Introduction* (New York: Oxford University Press, 1996), pp. 16–27; Jonathan

Landaw and Janet Brooke, *Prince Siddhartha: The Story of Buddha,* (Boston: Wisdom, 1984), pp. 46–69; and Donald S. Lopez Jr., *The Story of Buddhism: A Concise Guide to Its History and Teachings* (San Francisco: HarperSanFrancisco, 2001), pp. 37–42, 54–56.

56 *the ordinary, unenlightened human life* My use of the word *unenlightened* in articulating the First Noble Truth comes from Robert A. F. Thurman, "Boardroom Buddhism," *Civilization,* Dec. 1999–Jan. 2000, p. 61. Thanks to Jonathan Strom for calling my attention to this issue of *Civilization.*

57 *Ecclesiastes* The references in this paragraph are to Ecclesiastes 1–5. Thanks to Brian Mahan for pointing out some of the similarities between Ecclesiastes and Zen.

57 *Augustine* Saint Augustine, *Confessions,* trans. R. S. Pine-Coffin (New York: Penguin, 1961), pp. 75–78.

58 *when desire is possessive* I picked up the helpful distinction between desire and possessive desire from Denys Turner, *The Darkness of God: Negativity in Christian Mysticism* (New York: Cambridge University Press, 1995), pp. 183–184.

59 *True satisfaction is found . . .* This sentence is inspired by Sylvia Boorstein's articulation of the Second Noble Truth in *It's Easier Than You Think: The Buddhist Way to Happiness* (San Francisco: HarperSanFrancisco, 1995), p. 19.

60 *"It does not do . . ."* J.R.R. Tolkien, *The Hobbit* (Boston: Houghton Mifflin, 1999).

62 *selflessness is not alien to Christianity* Quotes from Paul: Galatians 2:20; Romans 12:5. *Love your neighbor as yourself:* Leviticus 19:18; Matthew 19:19, 22:39; Mark 12:31; Luke 10:27; Romans 13:9; Galatians 5:14; James 2:8.

62 *"If I loved my neighbour . . ."* Lewis, *Letters to Malcolm,* pp. 114–115.

62 *selflessness doesn't mean . . . we shouldn't use the word* I   This idea is from Paul Williams, *Mahayana Buddhism: The Doctrinal Foundations* (New York: Routledge, 1989), p. 67.

63 *two levels of truth*   I borrowed this phrase from H. H. the Dalai Lama and Alexander Berzin, *The Gelug/Kagyü Tradition of Mahamudra* (Ithaca, N.Y.: Snow Lion, 1997), p. 160.

63 *(Much of the paradoxical-sounding rhetoric . . .)*   This idea is from Williams, *Mahayana Buddhism,* p. 46.

64 *"His students . . ."*   Philip Martin, *The Zen Path Through Depression* (San Francisco: HarperSanFrancisco, 1999), p. 20.

64 *"Pain is inevitable, but suffering is optional."*   This is Sylvia Boorstein's articulation of the First Noble Truth in *It's Easier Than You Think,* p. 16. The phrase "Suffering is optional" is also used by Zen teacher Cheri Huber, *Suffering Is Optional* (Mountain View, Calif.: Keep It Simple Books, 2000).

65 *"Third-and-a-Half Noble Truth": "Suffering is manageable"*   Boorstein, *It's Easier Than You Think,* p. 26.

65 *Eightfold Path*   For the discussion of the Eightfold Path, I have drawn especially on Corless, *The Vision of Buddhism,* pp. 210–211; Lama Surya Das, *Awakening the Buddha Within* (New York: Broadway Books, 1997); Walpola Rahula, *What the Buddha Taught* (New York: Grove Press, 1974), pp. 45–50; and the entries on the "Eightfold Path" and "trishiksha" (the Three Trainings) in *The Shambhala Dictionary of Buddhism and Zen* (Boston: Shambhala, 1991).

65 *"skillful" and "realistic"*   "Skillful": Bhante Henepola Gunaratana, *Eight Mindful Steps to Happiness: Walking the Buddha's Path* (Boston: Wisdom, 2001). "Realistic": Thurman, "Boardroom Buddhism," p. 61.

69 *A student complained to the Buddha . . .*   The story of the poisoned arrow is condensed and paraphrased from Rahula, *What the Buddha Taught,* pp. 12–15.

Practice: Noticing Thoughts

73 *not about eliminating thoughts but illuminating them*   I got this phrase from a meditation instructor at the Shambhala Meditation Center of Atlanta. He didn't know where he'd gotten it.

76 *"To study the Buddha Way . . ."*   From Dogen's *Genjokoan*. A slightly different translation appears in Kazuaki Tanahashi (ed.), *Moon in a Dewdrop: Writings of Zen Master Dogen* (New York: North Point Press, 1985), p. 70.

77 *precise but also gentle*   I have borrowed these adjectives from Pema Chödrön, "Precision, Gentleness, and Letting Go," in *The Wisdom of No Escape: And the Path of Lovingkindness* (Boston: Shambhala, 1991), pp. 13–20.

77 *You're at a train station*   I got the train station image from a meditation instructor connected with the Naropa Institute (now Naropa University) or Shambhala Training in Boulder, Colorado, in the late 1980s; I don't remember now who it was.

78 *let it be*   I more often hear the instruction to "let thoughts go," but I like the idea of "letting thoughts be," which I found in Joseph Goldstein, *Insight Meditation: The Practice of Freedom* (Boston: Shambhala, 1993), pp. 39–41.

78 *Hug each thought goodbye*   Thanks to Laurie Watel for the phrase "hugging thoughts goodbye" to succinctly capture the train station image.

79 *If it seems like it was one big blur . . .*   The idea in this sentence came from Beck, *Everyday Zen,* pp. 26–27.

79 *When Jesus says . . .*   Matthew 5:27–28.

79 *"Be angry but do not sin"*   Ephesians 4:26a.

79 *"Sometimes pious men and women . . ." and "There is no real danger . . ."*   Thomas Merton, *New Seeds of Contemplation* (New York: New Directions, 1961), pp. 222–223.

Chapter Three: Zen Teachings and Christian Teachings

83 *This is a koan . . .*   Koan quoted from Paul Reps and Nyogen Senzaki (eds.), *Zen Flesh, Zen Bones: A Collection of Zen and Pre-Zen Writings* (Boston: Tuttle, 1998), p. 155.

85 *Nonduality negates twoness . . .*   That "nonduality" negates twoness without affirming oneness was first made clear to me in the chapter "The Buddhist-Christian Dialogue" in David Tracy's *Dialogue with the Other* (Grand Rapids, Mich.: Eerdmans, 1990), p. 69. See also Williams, *Mahayana Buddhism,* pp. 63–65.

87 *George Lindbeck*   Quotations from George Lindbeck, *The Nature of Doctrine: Religion and Theology in a Postliberal Age* (Louisville, Ky.: Westminster/John Knox, 1984), pp. 16–17. (Lindbeck proposes understanding doctrines in a fourth way, as "communally authoritative rules of discourse, attitude, and action." This "cultural-linguistic" approach emphasizes the similarities between religion and language.)

89 *things are a big mess, but it's OK anyway*   This idea and its phrasing were inspired by the chapter "It's OK" in Charlotte Joko Beck's *Everyday Zen,* pp. 114–118, and by the statement, "Practice is about finally understanding the paradox that although everything is a mess, all is well," in Ezra Bayda, "What Practice Is," *Zen Center of San Diego Newsletter,* Jan. 1996, which is available on-line at www.prairiezen.org /archive/practice.htm.

95 *"by grace alone . . ." and "We confess together . . ."*   Roman Catholic Church and Lutheran World Federation, "Joint Declaration on the Doctrine of Justification," 1999, paragraphs 15 and 37, available on-line at www.elca.org/ea/ Ecumenical/romancatholic/jddj/jddj.html.

96 *a friend of mine asked me*   Thanks to Jan Thomas for this and other good theological conversations by e-mail.

99 *incommensurable* Thanks to Brian Mahan for pointing out that I should use three categories here instead of two—not just similarities and differences but also incommensurabilities—and for recommending that I read David Tracy's "The Buddhist-Christian Dialogue" and that I use Lindbeck's categories in this chapter.

100 *"neither are we two, . . ."* Tracy, *Dialogue with the Other*, p. 94.

Chapter Four: Enlightenment: Already and Not Yet

109 *Issan Dorsey* This story is drawn from Kobai Scott Whitney, "The Lone Mountain Path: The Example of Issan Dorsey," *Shambhala Sun,* Mar. 1998.

111 *"Let me respectfully . . ."* "Evening Gatha," in John Daido Loori (ed.), *Zen Mountain Monastery Liturgy Manual* (Mt. Tremper, N.Y.: Dharma Communications, 1998), p. 47.

111 *practice meditation as if your hair is on fire* From Dogen's *Zazen-gi (Rules for Zazen)* and *Gakudo Yojin-shu (Guidelines for Studying the Way).* See Tanahashi, *Moon in a Dewdrop,* pp. 29, 31.

112 *Bodhidharma and Hui-k'o* For these stories, I have drawn on Heinrich Dumoulin, *Zen Buddhism: A History:* Vol. 1, *India and China,* trans. James W. Heisig and Paul Knitter (Old Tappan, N.J.: Macmillan, 1988), p. 92; Nelson Foster and Jack Shoemaker (eds.), *The Roaring Stream: A New Zen Reader* (Hopewell, N.J.: Ecco Press, 1996), pp. 6–8; Alan W. Watts, *The Way of Zen* (New York: Pantheon, 1957), pp. 91–92; and the entries "Bodhidharma" and "Hui-k'o" in *The Shambhala Dictionary of Buddhism and Zen* and in Charles S. Prebish (ed.), *Historical Dictionary of Buddhism* (Metuchen, N.J.: Scarecrow Press, 1993).

113 *one historian* Kenneth Ch'en, *Buddhism in China: A Historical Survey* (Princeton, N.J.: Princeton University Press, 1964), p. 352.

114 *"like some sort of goblin . . ."* Hakuun Yasutani, *Flowers Fall,* trans. Paul Jaffe (Boston: Shambhala, 1996), p. 43.

114 *This paradoxical language* I was assisted in understanding and articulating this point—that paradox is a way to use language to point beyond language—by Turner, *The Darkness of God,* ch. 2.

115 *"For us, complete perfection . . ."* Suzuki, *Zen Mind, Beginner's Mind,* p. 103.

116 *riding around on your ox* Yasutani, *Flowers Fall,* p. 42.

117 *"The ogre outside . . ."* Hakuin, *Zen Words for the Heart: Hakuin's Commentary on the Heart Sutra,* trans. Norman Waddell (Boston: Shambhala, 1996), p. 24.

121 *bodhisattva* For the definition of a bodhisattva, I have drawn on Corless, *The Vision of Buddhism,* pp. 41–42; and the "bodhisattva" entries in *The Shambhala Dictionary of Buddhism and Zen* and Prebish, *Historical Dictionary of Buddhism.* The second definition is from Donald S. Lopez Jr., *The Heart Sutra Explained* (Albany: State University of New York Press, 1988), p. 39.

124 Getting Saved from the Sixties Steven M. Tipton, *Getting Saved from the Sixties* (Berkeley: University of California Press, 1982).

124 *a similar way of understanding Christian morality* Lewis, *Letters to Malcolm,* pp. 114–115.

Practice: Practicing with Everything

128 *a Korean Baptist seminary professor* Thanks to Gerald May for sharing this story.

Chapter Five: Making Zen Practice
Part of Your Life

141 *Form, or physical reality, is empty* The interpretation of "Form is emptiness; emptiness is form" in this sentence comes from Lopez, *The Heart Sutra Explained*, p. 72.

141 *"no suffering, . . ." and "far beyond deluded thoughts"* "The Heart Sutra," in Loori, *Zen Mountain Monastery Liturgy Manual*, p. 27.

142 *Four Bodhisattva Vows* Translation used by the Atlanta Soto Zen Center, Atlanta.

145 *"dark to the mind but radiant to the heart"* John Daido Loori, *Mountain Record of Zen Talks* (Boston: Shambhala, 1988), p. xiii.

146 *More than half* This is suggested by James William Coleman, "The New Buddhism: Some Empirical Findings," in Duncan Ryuken Williams and Christopher S. Queen (eds.), *American Buddhism: Methods and Findings in Recent Scholarship* (Surrey, England: Curzon Press, 1999), pp. 94–95.

148 sesshin *and* shin The translations of these terms are from the entries on "sesshin" and "kokoro" (*shin*) in *The Shambhala Dictionary of Buddhism and Zen.*

Practice: Zazen: *Shikantaza*, or "Just Sitting"

151 *"nothing but precisely sitting"* This is the literal translation of *shikantaza* given in *The Shambhala Dictionary of Buddhism and Zen.*

154 *"You must sit . . ."* Hakuun Yasutani, in Philip Kapleau, *The Three Pillars of Zen* (New York: Doubleday, 1980), p. 128.

157 *"it-doesn't-matter Zen . . ."* Yasutani, *Flowers Fall*, p. 19.

One More Thought: If It's Worth Doing, It's Worth Doing Badly

159 *"The Joys of Mediocrity"* Linda Weltner, "The Joys of Mediocrity: Anything Worth Doing Is Worth Doing Badly," *Utne Reader,* Jan.-Feb. 1994, pp. 99–100, reprinted from *New Age Journal*, Sept.-Oct. 1993.

160 *"If a thing is worth doing, . . ."* G. K. Chesterton, *What's Wrong with the World* (New York: Dodd, Mead, 1910).

160 *"requires the humility . . ."* David Yount, *Breaking Through God's Silence* (Touchstone Books, 1997).

160 *"It's been my observation . . ."* Fred Craddock, "Cloud of Witnesses," audiotape of a sermon given on May 25, 1985 (Atlanta: Candler School of Theology Media Center, Emory University, 1985).

Acknowledgments

Thanks especially to my husband, Brian Mahan—my primary conversation partner about Zen, Christianity, theology, spiritual formation, religious education, and writing—whose influence permeates the content, structure, and style of this book. In particular, I am indebted to Brian for my understanding of the centrality in spiritual practice of attending to what *inhibits* us from living with wisdom and compassion.

Thanks to Gerald May, who has shaped my whole way of understanding contemplative practice, both Buddhist and Christian. Thanks to Laurie Watel and Jennifer Watts for our conversations about religion, theology, and spiritual practice and for sharing my excitement about this project. To Anne Mushin Kaufhold: Happy sixteenth anniversary of our spring break at the monastery!

For excellent editing, I am grateful to Sheryl Fullerton at Jossey-Bass. For reading the manuscript and offering helpful feedback, I am grateful to Tom Frank, E. Brooks Holifield, Wynne Maggi, Brian Mahan, Steve Tipton, Bonnie Myotai Treace, and Laurie Watel. Thanks to Luke Timothy Johnson, Eric Reinders, and Neal Walls for looking over particular sections of the manuscript. Thanks to Bruce Emmer and Fred

Helenius for copyediting and proofreading. Thanks to Tom Beaudoin for help with the publishing game, and thanks to my dad and stepmom, Noel and Robin Boykin, and my mom, Karin Paris, for the computer and printer. And thanks to everyone at Jossey-Bass who worked on this book.

Thanks to Jan Thomas, Derek Owens, Jennifer Watts, and my dad for e-mail conversations that led to drafts of sections of the book and to the scholars and staff of the Youth Theology Institute for all the great theological conversations by e-mail. Thanks to Jim Fowler for many kinds of support over the past decade and to Michael Warren for encouragement at the beginning of this project. I am grateful for Anne Lamott's *Bird by Bird* and V. A. Howard and J. H. Barton's *Thinking on Paper;* I don't think I would have been able to write a book without their help.

For getting me started leading Zen meditation groups for Christians, I am grateful to the Shalem Institute for Spiritual Formation. For opportunities to lead Zen groups and for their encouragement, I am grateful to Mary-Elizabeth Ellard, Budd Friend-Jones, and Helen Neinast. For other teaching opportunities, I am grateful to Carolyn Barker, John Barnes, Beth Luton Cook, Tom Curtis, Taiun Michael Elliston, Jim Farwell, Jerry Kane, Mari Kim-Shinn, Victor Kramer, Alison Mallard, Ellen Mintzmyer, Amy Murphy, Don Richter, Fred Rossini, Sue Sherwood, Dennis Teall-Fleming, Mark Monk Winstanley, and the Evening at Emory program. And I am grateful to all the wonderful participants in my classes and meditation groups.

My understanding of how to practice meditation and how to teach meditation to beginners has been shaped by many teachers, in person and through their writing, but especially by John Daido Loori, Bonnie Myotai Treace, and the other monastics at Zen Mountain Monastery; by Philip Kapleau's *The Three Pillars of Zen,* especially the teachings of Hakuun Yasutani; by Charlotte Joko Beck's *Everyday Zen;* by the writings of Chögyam Trungpa; and by the meditation instructors of Naropa University and Shambhala Training. I am grateful also to Sister Eleanor Sheehan, Fay Key, and Gerald May for spiritual guidance and to Roberta Bondi, Bill Mallard, and Helen Blier for Christian catechism.

And finally, special thanks to Fay Key and Steve Bullington of Green Bough House of Prayer, where I did most of the work on this book, for providing a place of prayer and silence and for hospitality, love, and good food.

The Author

Kim Boykin (M.T.S., Candler School of Theology, Emory University) is a Christian practitioner of Zen and an experienced workshop leader and teacher of Zen practices and contemplative prayer, to both Christian and non-Christian audiences. She has written for a number of publications, including *Shambhala Sun*.

Index

Other Books of Interest

Embracing the World: *Praying for Justice and Peace*

Jane E. Vennard

$18.95 Cloth

ISBN: 0-7879-5887-5

A wise, helpful and nourishing book, filled with personal stories and practical guidance.
—**Marcus J. Borg**, author, *Meeting Jesus Again for the First Time* and *Reading the Bible Again for the First Time*

Jane Vennard's carefully constructed book creates much-needed bridges—between the personal and political, the mystical and mundane, the pastoral and prophetic—so that pilgrims can connect to the world and beyond.
—**Swanee Hunt**, former United States Ambassador to Austria

Prayer is not a detached, abstract spiritual practice but a way of engaging with the world. This book is for those who not only want a deeper relationship with God through prayer, but who also want to believe their prayers can make a difference and empower them to feel they are helping to contribute to a better world. Looking at prayer in its broadest form—as both contemplation *and* action—Jane Vennard guides readers in how to use their gifts and graces to serve God and the cause of peace and social justice here on earth. Through description, explanation, stories, and biblical and theological reflections, Vennard explores in detail many different forms of outward-reaching prayer. She offers a practical guide for creating a prayer and action cycle where prayer leads to service and service leads to reflection and back to God. *Embracing the World* is for everyone—activist and contemplative—who cares about making the world a better place.

JANE E. VENNARD is the author of three previous books on prayer and is a popular speaker, retreat leader, teacher, and spiritual director. This book grows out of her teaching of a course by the same name at Iliff School of Theology in Denver, where she witnessed first-hand the many shifts in her students' lives as they began to focus their prayer in a new way and to discern what actions they might take that would promote justice and peace in the world around them.

[Price subject to change]

Hearing with the Heart: A Gentle Guide to Discerning God's Will for Your Life

Debra K. Farrington

$19.95 Cloth ISBN: 0–7879–5959–6

What does God wish for you in your life? How do you listen for God's gracious guidance as you face daily decisions, both big and small? And how do you know that what you are hearing comes from God and not your ego or simply your own wishful thinking?

Only through learning to hear with our hearts tuned closely to God can we discern how we should find our way through the crowded and confusing thickets of our lives. In *Hearing with the Heart,* popular writer and retreat leader Debra Farrington leads you through a gentle process for discovering how to invite God's presence into every aspect of your daily life. Her story-filled discussions of key practices such as prayer, meditation, reading and reflection, and attentiveness to your body, your studies, and your relationships with your friends and family, help you discover how to be open to discerning God's will. Filled with a wealth of exercises, guidelines, and tools, *Hearing with the Heart* gives you the practical help you need to bring you closer to God. As you put these suggestions into practice you will find yourself opening more and more to God's infinite possibilities for you.

Hearing with the Heart samples a broad range of stories taken from the Bible, classic and contemporary literature, and everyday experiences. It can be an indispensable resource for discerning how to proceed at major crossroads and navigate life's challenges at work, in relationships, or during crisis situations and how to truly be partners with God in creating your life. This gentle and compassionate companion for helping to reveal God's hopes and desires for you will not only bring joy to your life but also to the lives of others and to a world where peace, love, and charity can flourish.

Learning to Hear with the Heart: Meditations for Discerning God's Will

Debra K. Farrington

$15.95 Hardcover   ISBN: 0–7879–6716–5

Suitable as both a companion book to *Hearing with the Heart* and as a stand-alone, this inspirational guide to the discernment process can be used for individual devotional reading as well as small group work. However it is used, *Learning to Hear with the Heart* will help readers find their way to the truth of their lives by learning to listen for the still, small voice.

DEBRA K. FARRINGTON—an insightful writer and popular retreat leader—is publisher of Morehouse Publishing and the former manager of the Graduate Theological Union Bookstore in Berkeley, California. Farrington has written for a wide variety of publications including *Spirituality and Health, Catholic Digest, The Lutheran, Publishers Weekly, U.S. Catholic,* and many others.

[Prices subject to change]